Fund Your Company

Andrew D. Ive

Review

As an independent author, reviews are one of the most important ways I have to get the word out. I'd be in your debt if you'd consider writing your thoughts on this book in whichever site you bought it from. Your review will encourage others to grab the book.

Go to my author page here if you want to discuss any elements of the book or have follow up questions/thoughts (Author Page)

Published in United States by

Andrew D. Ive

www.AntPublishingHouse.com

**** Your Executive Summary Free Gift
http://www.AndrewIve.com/executivesummarygift

Table of Contents

CHAPTER ONE: Offering Help

Your 'Why?'

Whatever your motivations for starting your own company - Making a difference in the world. Pursuing your true purpose. Doing something cool. Working with great people. Making yourself wealthy. Lost your job, retired or just starting over. A passion for something - whichever reason is relevant to you, many people start amazing, exciting, life and world changing, successful and unsuccessful companies every day and recreate their lives and those of everyone they touch.

But whatever your personal reason for wanting to create your own company, getting the funds should not be a wall which stops you from starting your company.

I'll make that point one more time, a lack of cash in your company's bank account should not be the reason why your business doesn't start or grow.

Now let's unpack that point.

When I first went out to get funding for my first company, I did it while working a day job. At that time I'd graduated from the Harvard Business School with an MBA and had an extended network like you wouldn't believe - so guess how long it took me to raise my first investor funding? A week? A month? Six months?

I wish it have taken any of those.

The first time, with everything going for me, it took more than a year and it's worth sharing that I worked on my startup business every day - this wasn't a once every so often effort. I was driven, persistent and thought it was going to take a month or two at most.

Hindsight is a Bitch

A few years since that time has given me the benefit of hindsight. It was a year or two after I'd moved on from that company before I sat down and dissected exactly why it took me that length of time and that insight came about by accident. Having returned for a year or two to the United Kingdom, the UK government asked me to sit on a Board of the Department of Trade and Industry, to advise on how to make the country more entrepreneurial. The department had undertaken what they called, The Big Survey. This was a survey of all companies in the United Kingdom, asking them about their businesses, challenges and opportunities.

The results of that study was in two parts - first, that there was no shortage of funding for companies and second, the reason why entrepreneurs and companies had challenges raising money was...because they weren't investment ready.

I was pissed when I was told that. Think about those two points for a second.

 i)   *There's plenty of money available for companies but the reason why they don't*
       get the money is because they ii) aren't ready to take it.

As an entrepreneur who had spent more than a year looking for investors, this study was saying I'd spent all that time unsuccessfully raising money, because I and my startup wasn't ready or developed enough to get the investors to say "Yes".

How dare they!?!?! I was completely pis…

Then, like a plank upside my head, I got it.

Crap! No - I hadn't been ready during most of that year raising money…

Damn they were right…

Over the next month I really broke down where I and my business had been when we first starting raising money and where it was (and our pitch had got too) when we got our first $250,000 from our angel investors. Yes I had spent a year looking for money before getting my investors but I hadn't sat and waited while I waited for the money, I had moved my business forward. Moving it forward to the point where investors were prepared to risk their hard earned money on me and my business.

Does this mean you will find it near impossible to raise money for your business?

No - that's to why I wrote the above paragraph - the points I'd like you to take away are i) there are funds available to you but ii) you and your business have to be truly ready to get the funds. Now to be ready does not mean wanting funding, being desperate for funding or needing funding. It means being aware of the sources of funding and what you need to show and provide to be able to secure that funding.

As someone who has raised funds from various sources I'd like to share that it's neither easy not impossible to raise money for your business - to raise that money, a few important considerations….

You need to know the most appropriate funding sources for your stage of business, how to reach out and engage them, what those sources need so they can make a decision. Then you need to go do it.

That's what this book is about.

There are a variety of ways to get funding for your business. This book will take you through some of the main ways, take you through some of the nuances, and the watch outs.

IMPORTANT:

When writing this book I'm not bringing together a variety of definitions for academic purposes. Sure I could go to dictionary.com or Wikipedia and start pulling the 'academic' definition of everything but my purpose is to give you a real world view – For example, if you want to know how angel investors are defined, by all means head over to one of those sources and read all about them.

No - what this book is about is the real world practical (and personal) insights regarding each of these sources. The definitions, thoughts and suggestions are all mine based on my experiences working with these different funding sources and other entrepreneurs to get funding. I'm sure I've made mistakes and they'll be academic folks who will disagree with my definitions and suggestions - they're welcome to do so. I may even take the good suggestions on-board.

However, the person I most want feedback from is you. After reading through this book - I'd like to hear from YOU. If you have suggestions, questions or feedback – Reach out. This is the first edition – they'll be mistakes and omissions. Let me know via andrewive.com *or* thefundingguru.com.

You can find more tools we've created to help entrepreneurs just like you from my website that was named and created way before gurus got a bad name:

http://www.TheFundingGuru.com

CHAPTER TWO: Overview

Something for Nothing?

You rarely get something for nothing and the same is true for funding.

The important questions are 'what do you have to give to get the funding you need for your business?' and 'is it worth it to you?'

In this book I'll take you through the main ways entrepreneurs are funding their new companies. The list is not all inclusive but I'd like to bet that 95% of all new companies use one of the methods we cover to get started in this book to start and grow their businesses. By reading this book you'll understand some of the key opportunities and maybe pitfalls to avoid.

In each case we'll go through the most common things you should understand before pursuing the funding source, including what you will need to 'give' to get the funding. What this book can't do is tell you what is a good or a bad deal for you - you'll need to decide that for yourself, maybe after taking individual advice from an expert. You are welcome to reach out to me if you have questions - you'll find my email and contact details at the front of the book.

Here are a few examples of what you will typically need to "give to get" some of the funding outlined:

1) Venture Capital (VC's) - will most usually be looking to gain equity (the word we'll use to describe shares or units) in the companies they invest in, perhaps they'll want a seat on your board and there will be other requests in the term sheet you'll need to negotiate. A term sheet is the document which summarizes the terms of the deal they're proposing.

2) Angel Investors - Often look for equity in the companies they support, expect regular updates and like VC's, they'll have terms they'll want to negotiate with you - such as the right to purchase equity at future rounds of investment. They may also propose convertible notes rather than or in addition to a straight equity purchase – a convertible note is an agreement usually structured so the angel investors received the same type of shares as the next round of investors, but at a pre-agreed discount to the price set in the next round.

3) Crowd Funding – Funders of crowd funding campaigns will look for perks or rewards. As this is not giving up shares or taking on debt, crowd funding can be a great way to get started if you have a product or service which could be appealing to a passionate group of target-able potential customers.

To understand the key elements of all the funding types, take a look at the respective types we've separated into chapters.

Don't Forget - You Always Have Choices

Even if you don't have money right now, there's one thing you DO have as an entrepreneur, a founder, and as CEO and that's 'Choice'.

It's your business - you have choices, that's what being the founder and CEO is all about. It's up to you to make the decisions - the good and bad. You can decide how you fund your business and if you use someone else's money, who's money and under what conditions. You are never forced into it - you can always walk away. Sure walking away has consequences, but you still have choice. Don't forget it and try not to give up that ability.

If we meet in real life, remind me to tell you when I told a VC that we wouldn't be accepting their $6M under their (horrible) terms and they could go to hell. At the time we had salaries and rent to pay and no other funding ready to close. As the terms were so onerous, I sat down with my team and took them through the whole deal, asking them what we (together) should do next. They thought it through then told me to tell the VCs to take a hike. I did just that.

You always have the choice of whether you will or will not look for or accept funding. Then, if you find some available funding, whether you'll accept the terms or wait.

Please remember that point.

Many entrepreneurs I've worked with get into desperation mode when going out to raise funding. They start seeing their success (or not) in raising money as the indicator of whether or not they'll be able to start their company and whether or not it will be successful.

REMEMBER: Some of the best businesses have been boot-strapped without outside funding at all.

Try not to see the existence of outside cash as the Go or No go button that you must press. It isn't.

The best way to start your business is to start it.

If you don't have resources, time to get resourceful.

Easy to say (or write) and tough as hell to actually do. But one thing you'll need as a great founder is mind numbing tenacity and the ability to find your way around obstacles – even when everyone, perhaps even your loved ones, are telling you to quit. Yes, that's two things but that's just me bending the rules – you should too ;)

Don't let investors tell you whether your business is worth it or worthy of life or if you're insane for thinking there could even be a business here. Newsflash - you are insane by average or normal standards and who wants to be in that sane, normal, average category anyway…?

So start it, then prove it and the more you prove it, the more likely you'll be able to get funding.

The hardest business to get funded is one that's just on paper - an idea which has been read about but has not been explored.

Start your business. Please. Hell, pretty please even…

Go talk to those people who would be great customers and listen to what they tell you after you tell them about your business. The more you talk, listen, iterate (important point – be prepared to pivot) and evolve your business - the more you are proving that it deserves funding. Then go get it.

And use the insights you've gained from would-be customers to support your pitch.

Funding means getting cash that you can use to start and or grow your business.

We're going to focus on the main sources of funding available for a company, what they are, their pros and cons and what you usually need to be able to secure that type of funding.

In each case I've raised money through these different sources so we'll go through some of the benefits and challenges directly.

Over the last ten or so years I've also coached a number of startup founders who have also funded themselves using these approaches - you are gaining the benefit of multiple data points

Whichever funding source you consider - there is always more to the deal than just receiving the money. Rarely can you raise money without taking on additional responsibilities. Example - when you take on a loan you take on debt. You must repay the loan at specific times and at a specific rate of interest. Likewise if you raise money by selling equity in your company to an investor - you have just gained a partner (even if a minor partner) on your business.

The purpose of this book is to take you through the most usual methods for funding startups and some of the consequences and considerations from these methods.

Take on-board that not all funding sources are right for and available to you right now.

Why can't I pursue all these funding sources?

Well you can try, but you'll likely be unsuccessful and would waste a hell of a lot of your time. The funding sources we cover are the most relevant to most business but how relevant will depend on what you and your company have achieved and which industry you are in. Not all the funding sources are right for every business.

Why is that?

There's an important concept in business called life cycle. A business which is completely new, little more than a business plan and a few conversations with customers is a new business. A new business has a different set of characteristics than a mature business, with a full team, consistent customers, growing revenues and a proven business model.

In the first example - the company that is only days or weeks old is considered risky. It still has a long way to go from a concept being validated in the market, to a real growing business with revenues. Here's a potential 'A Ha' moment for you…the less risky a company is, the more money you should be able to secure for it. It isn't necessarily fair or smart - some companies which are risky, can be the most exciting for investors but only because the investors are weighing the risk versus the reward and want more of the company to take the risk.

If you are looking to gain funding then one of your key roles is to move your business forward while you go through funding to reduce the uncertainty around your business model. The lower the uncertainty, the easier for you to gain strong investors, customers and employees.

If your company is young consider focusing your funding efforts on sources such as self-funding, friends and family, customers and perhaps crowd sourcing. Likewise, if your company that has made significant progress, has many of the pieces necessary for growth and achieved significant milestones, your business could be a potential candidate for angel investors, VC, loans and / or strategic partnerships.

When considering the different funding sources, take your company's life cycle stage into consideration to identify the types of funding sources you should focus on.

Are there Exceptions to Life Cycle Alignment?
It's you choice. There are exceptions to everything right? But if time is precious to you, consider focusing on those sources which are focused on companies for your stage and type. I'll outline this for each funding source.

Consider Industry and Geography
The funding sources we're focused on have different levels of relative ease based on a few factors such as industry and geography.

For example - it's relatively easy to find angel investors in San Francisco, New York, Boston and London as there is a well developed network of successful entrepreneurs and business people who are actively looking to fund new, exciting, growing companies. That's not to say you'll be able to get them to back your company but it's obviously easier to hunt for deer in a forest filed with deer than to hunt for them in the desert.

Likewise, there is a well-developed ecosystem of entrepreneurs, businesses, angel investors and VCs focused on the technology, or biotech or clean tech industries versus the food or retail industries. There are VCs and Angels focused on investing in food and retail companies, however, there are far fewer than the tech industries.

Can you get funding if your business is not in one of the prime locations or Industries?

Yes - but it's more challenging. Having spent the last two years in Buffalo NY, not known for its highly developed entrepreneurial ecosystem, there are companies in Buffalo getting funded by angels, crowd funding, grants and VCs. We'll touch on why in the section focused on Angel investors but if you are not in Silicon Valley, Silicon Alley, Boston or London - don't buy your bus ticket quite yet, there are ways to gain funding outside of these developed entrepreneurial ecosystems.

So to wrap up funding life cycle alignment, the type of funding appropriate for your business will change as your business achieves more milestones. I'll mention which is appropriate (in most cases) at the beginning of each chapter. Keep in mind the earlier chapters in this book are likely to be more relevant to companies at their earliest stages and so on, but make your own determination. Remember - It's your choice.

A company achieves different milestones as it starts and grows. A milestone relates to an achievement. They are the markers that show you and others the progress the company is making. Milestones achieved relate to key aspects of the business such as customers, revenue, recruitment, product development, product launch and so on.

As you achieve more milestones, the easier it is to gain funding.

The more and bigger the milestones, the more you are proving your business model, your capabilities and the demand for your product or service. Achieve milestones, prove your business and reduce risks for investors, customers and employees.

The initial stages tend to focus on proving the business model, the next tend to focus on proving the system you've put in place can consistently deliver and capture the value, and the later stages focus on scaling to capture larger shares of your market.

Some typical Milestones:

Customers

- Your first beta customer
- Your first paying customer
- Customers acquired regularly, consistently and predictably

Team Building:

- Founder
- Recruited Co-Founder / s
- Recruit key team members

Product:

- Concept tested with customers / focus group
- Beta product launched to beta customers
- First version of product launched

Why are Milestones Important?

All investors have their own degree of comfort with risk. As you prove your business, the risk should be reduced. Also as investors have their own areas of expertise, what data points one investor might need to make a decision on opportunity and risk may be very different than another investor. That's when their personal areas of expertise and experience begin to factor into their decision or not to invest. Given this point, I always try to understand why an investor decides to not invest (or to pass) on my opportunities.

If a potential investor decides not to invest, instead of quickly rolling onto the next investor, do yourself a favor and circle back to understand why they decided to pass. Maybe given their experience, they know something I don't. Also, if they see an issue you don't, it's smart to understand that issue so you can address it with the next investor and dig deeper to understand if they're issue is valid or incorrect.

As this is your passion you'll likely jump to "the investor doesn't know what they're talking about..." - don't fall for it. Ignorance is not bliss, you need to understand your business better than anyone else on the planet.

You need to understand your business better than anyone else on the planet.

If one investor sees an issue, others will too. Understand and then get data to prove or disprove this belief. If you prove the issue does exist - find a way to fix or mitigate it. If this happens the investor who passed just did you a big favor - they told you about an issue others will spot and, by identifying it, they helped you to solve something which could have cause you problems after funding.

Why Should You Get Funding?

The reality is I don't always recommend you should *always* get funding.

Funding should be used strategically and at the appropriate time to help achieve your goals.

Use funding to speed up your time to market, to penetrate a new market, to launch a new product line, to beat the competition and grab profitable market share.

The longer you can go without selling equity (a word used to describe shares / units) or taking on debt in your company while achieving tangible milestones in your business, the better. Why?

Because the more value you can create in your business before taking on that equity, the more of that value you get to keep when you do fund your business through angels, VC or other funding sources.

For example - If you are looking to raise $1M and if your company is realistically worth $2M then you need to give up a big chunk of that business to get that $1M. However, if you have customers, revenues, a good rate of predictable growth in an exciting market then you may be able to make the case that your business is worth more than $2M - the higher the justifiable valuation, the less of your company you'll need to sell to investors to secure that $1M.

If you are looking for funding to start a company or to stay alive then your negotiating position is weak. The more proof you can get for your business, the higher the valuation and the less you need to give to investors to get them to invest.

A few Considerations When Raising Money:

It will take far longer than you expect to raise the money you need.

I rarely (if ever) hear from entrepreneurs that it took them far less time to find their ideal investors, to negotiate the ideal deal and close it.

Your Estimates Are Probably Wrong

The estimate you make in terms of delivering the product or service to market is usually an order of magnitude larger than you expect. Also the estimated time to start the company and deliver those beta products and services are also usually way off.

A rule of thumb is take your initial estimate of costs and double them - then take your best, most reasonable estimate of how long it will take to launch and double that too. And if that isn't pessimistic enough, take the amount you think you're going to sell in your first year and halve it.

If the economics still work, use those estimates when you go out to pitch investors and if you can lock in investors under those conditions, if you were too pessimistic, you can all have a big party when you blow those numbers out of the water and then send me a postcard.

CHAPTER THREE: The Case for Raising Money

The advantages of raising money:

Well…there's the money of course :)

Cash is the oxygen companies need to survive.

Your goal when starting and growing a business should be to bring cash into the company quickly and predictably. The reason why entrepreneurs will often consider the sources in this book is they can be short cuts to bringing in that cash - the cash needed for salaries, materials, space and whatever else your company needs to create value for your customers.

Funding is useful when starting a company and to grow your business. If your revenues cover the costs of doing business but do not leave a significant amount over for re-investment or growth then these funding sources can be leveraged to grow or, in some cases, even step change your business.

Funding can give their owners the ability to grow the business so they can increase market share; funding can help them scale and gain the benefits of being larger through purchasing, brand awareness and customer contracts. Being a significant player in an industry has advantages and funding can help your speed to market, your growth in market and your expansion into new and related markets. Funding, when used correctly, is a strategic advantage for new and old businesses.

However, when you take funding from a source, there are consequences and it's smart to be aware of the pros and cons.

For example, angel investors, when investing in a business, are often purchasing equity in your company. They are now shareholders/owners of your business. They will expect to be kept up to date on progress, perhaps involved in key decision making, especially future deals and investments you might want to make.

BONUS: To download a mind map of the 3 Critical 'Must Haves' for your first Investor Meeting - come to http://www.AndrewIve.com/3musthaves

CHAPTER FOUR: Self-Funding

SNAPSHOT

Self-Funding

Description:

As you would expect, self-funding is all about using your own funds to start your company and test your initial concept with your target audience. Some founders using savings to start and grow their company. Others may use credit cards or fund it by working another job and using part of their salary to get it started.

The Investment Amount Sweet Spot:

Companies have been started by founders on a zero budget. Founders have also taken their personal savings, even re-mortgaged their homes to get started.

Stage of Company

Typically self-funding is used at the very earliest stages of a company's life. The founder bank rolls the start of the company - incorporating, pursue trademarks, patents or other forms of intellectual protection and ideally, talking to customers.

Types of Companies / Industries

All industries have had companies initially funded by the founders, even if it's just to get the ball rolling. In some cases, I've worked with entrepreneurs who self-fund their businesses and as they have strong credibility, are able to get initial commitments from customers. In these cases, those companies have even skipped the initial need for funding from angel investors and VCs. They have been able to use their own resources and bootstrap their companies to the point where they can acquire customers and gain revenue without outside funding.

What You Need to Pitch Yourself:

This might sound odd but if you are not prepared to invest your own money in your own concept, whether its savings or some other personal source, then should you really be considering going out and asking for an investment from friends, or family or angels?

FOUNDER'S TIP:

I recommend before you DO decide to invest in your own business - take some time to create a business case that you'd present to a potential investor, even though it's just for your own personal use.

Ask yourself (and fully answer) some important questions such as what are some of the risks? What are the resources you'll need to be able to start and grow your company? What are your own personal strengths and weaknesses and what do you need to do to supplement your weaknesses?

I'm not suggesting you go through this exercise to make you change your mind but instead to not go into it blindly. Entrepreneurs DO need grit, determination and a stick-to-it-ness that is almost inhuman. That does NOT mean entrepreneurs need to jump in blindly but rather entrepreneurs need to practically understand what they'll need to line up if they're going to be successful. Luck, courage and a willingness to persevere are important but so is knowing what you don't know and figuring out how to fill in the jigsaw puzzle through others.

You're Criteria for Investment:

This is for you to decide. What do YOU need to see and understand about your opportunity before you pursue it? Are you going to jump in, quit everything else and go full time on your company or will you start it more slowly, while you work a day job? Obviously these are all personal decisions. With my first company, I started it as a student - in that case I had my basic costs of living covered and was single. The personal risks were minimal.

You need to decide how much risk you are prepared to take when you start your company. There are many ways to test your business model and even get initial customers without spending 24/7 on the business.

FOUNDER'S TIP:

When I did go full time on my first business, I'm not sure (hand on heart) that I was that much more productive than when I needed to balance my hours between developing my business and other responsibilities. There's something to be said to having daily deadlines and needing to get specific tasks accomplished within a constrained time - it tends to make many of us more productive.

What Do You Get for This Type of Investment?

- **Equity:** By funding your own company, you get to keep all ownership (often called equity) in your company

- **Control:** By funding it yourself, you don't need to consider other people's opinions and do not need to give any percentages of the company to others.

- **Answer Questions:** By funding your own company, you can move your idea forward and answer some burning questions you have about it. Are customers truly interested? Are they actually prepared to put their hands in their pockets and pay for your product or service? Can you make a go of it yourself? Do you have what it takes to start a business and work for yourself? By starting the business, you get to answer some or perhaps all of these questions for yourself.

When You Want Your Investment Back?

If you fund your own company, when do you get your investment back?

You can gain funds from your company when you have revenues and profits. In that case you may decide to pay yourself a salary. A salary is not paying you back for your investment. That investment is usually paid back if you decide to sell the company or grow it to the point where you can take your company public. In both of those cases, the equity you own in your company, that you earned by starting the company and investing in it, may be able to be cashed out. If a company acquires your company for X, then you could receive the percentage of X that you owned in your own company when it was acquired.

FOUNDER'S NOTE:

The reason why I'm not definitively saying that's the case is that in some instances companies are acquired by the acquiring company giving their own stock to the shareholders of the acquired company rather than cash.

- Credit Cards
- Dipping into savings, retirement money
- Taking a percentage of wages from a job to cover initial startups costs and proof of concept

Benefits of Self-Funding

1. You are forced to focus on making money

When you have a shortage of money, this brings absolute clarity to what's critical in your business and what you need to be focusing your time and effort on. Sounds kinda scary but the day I stepped out of a very well-paying job and started my first company full time, although I had 100 things to do, it was immediately clear which of those 100 things needed my attention right now and which could wait - in short, bring money through the door, like, yesterday was the #1 focus.

At that time I started to see money in the bank as oxygen that was slowly but surely slipping through my fingers. You get an unbelievable clarity on how to spend your time and how to spend you limited resources.

2. You focus 100% on getting and delighting customers instead of getting investors

To some degree, although there are certainly shortcuts, raising money from investors is something of a numbers game. You might need to meet with 20 investors to get 3 or 4 who might be really interested in investing and only 1 of those might give you a term sheet. Scheduling, preparing for the meeting, meeting, following up and meeting some more with 20 investors take a huge amount of time.

If you are also learning HOW to go through that process through trial and error then it can take months - those months are not being spent getting and delighting customers, growing your market, improving your product, growing your business. Now the hope and expectation is the money you raise will speed up the business so that it's worth this funding time sink.

If and when you do decide to raise money - your goals should be to do so quickly, efficiently and to continue to move your business forward despite not having that funding yet.

3. You Are the Boss

Anyone who's ever worked for some else will know that a significant percentage of your time is spent proving yourself and legitimizing your place in the company. Performance reviews, face time, doing what you're told and all the other time sinks that come from being an employee all disappear when you work for yourself and you have very little money. You don't have to justify your existence to anyone except the customer. At the end of the day the customer pays your wages, not the person cutting the check and when you're the entrepreneur and can see that, wowing the customer is all that matters. Creating the best product, getting it into the hands of an excited customer and making sure they have a fantastic experience then tell their friends is the number one priority. And now that you are the boss - you can stop all the crap and the politics and dedicate yourself and the business you're building to making every customer an evangelist.

4. How to Spend Your Money Becomes Crystal Clear

When you have $1M in the bank from an investor which will cover your business for six month, nine months or a year - then you are not necessarily spending on the absolute necessities. But cut amount to $20K and you'll think hard about every dollar you spend - you'll be focused on making sure that every dollar works hard for your business.

When you self-fund, unless you are a trust fund baby, you'll be on a tight budget and have now entered the world of the boot-strapper. You are focused on making every dime count. You may not believe me but it's actually quite refreshing as it helps you cut through all the confusion and just do the important stuff - some people believe this approach will get you further faster than having investor money drowning you in cash.

5. Ethical and Less than Ethical People in Early Stage Funding

Not everyone in the funding ecosystem is a good, pleasant, giving, ethical person. Like any industry there are folks are would steal the pennies out of the pockets of a corpse. Self-funding means you get to surround yourself with the people you choose at all times. Sure you'll still need to keep your eyes open for those people who are less than ethical but startup funding has more than its fair share of dubious characters. A shame to say it, but it's true.

6. You Set The Pace

When you self-fund, you get to decide how quickly you grow, how many products or services you launch, how many customers you acquire - in short, you build your entire business at the pace that works for you and the resources available. When you have partners and investors, they'll have expectations about when they want their investments to pay out and how large they'll want that investment to be worth. In other words, investors will often drive the business to grow at the rate they believe is ideal - this may be contrary to the rate you believe is ideal.

7. Customer Satisfaction is #1

OK, perhaps customer satisfaction may not be #1 if you are self-funded and could very well be #1 if you are funded by investors, neither is exclusive to either scenario. However, if you have very little money and are self-funding, if you want to survive, you'll focus on making sure your first, second and one hundredth customers walk away overjoyed with their experience with you, your company and your products or services.

Zappos sell shoes that everyone sells, but their billions of customers talk about their customer service. That is what WOWs them and that is why Zappos became a billion dollar company. If you are self-funded, take care of your customers and they'll take care of you. If you are investor funded, take care of your customers and they'll take care of you.

8. Boot-strappers Unite

There's a pretty well developed community of founders who are bootstrapping their way to building some great companies. They are quite a supportive group of folks who will help each other.

Many of the cities I've spent time in have a well-developed network of meetups and equivalent where bootstrapping founders get together to share war stories, share contacts, experience and help each other along. If they're successful and growing it's because they're doing a lot of things right - they're growth is not driven by throwing dollars at a problem but getting their formula right.

If you decide to self-fund, get out there and look for other boot-strappers in your neighborhood. If there aren't any meetups created, start one and thank me later.

9. You work on a business that you are passionate about

When you self-fund, you set your direction and decide what the company focuses on. That's not always the case when you have investors as they're looking for growth, a return and building something huge. They're looking to get the company sold or across the $100M threshold (or whatever it is in your industry) so you can IPO. Those growth plans might work for you or they might not. As the self-funded founder, you get to decide.

10. You increase your leverage for future fundraising

The more proof you have for your business and its viability, the more leverage you have when you look to raise money from outside sources. By self-funding you give yourself more time and opportunity to prove viability. That gives you leverage.

Why Self Fund?

Keep More Of Your Business:

One of the most important lessons about funding is the more you prove your business model, the more value you are creating in your company. When (or if) you decide to raise money from external sources, the more real proof, justification, customer testimonials and milestones you've achieved, the less risk for investors. So the short answer is by funding your own company, you can make progress and move from 'idea' towards 'real business'. The more milestones you can achieve before you go out and raise money from others, the high the value of your company. The higher the value of your company before you raise money, the larger the amount you can raise for the equity you sell to investors.

If you put on the hat of an investor for a moment - would you be more likely to invest in a paper based business plan or in a company which already has customers, an in demand product, a leader, a team and a successful product launch?

Yeah, me too.

Keep Control of Your Business:

If you fund your business through any form of equity funding (Angels / VCs / Accelerators etc.) then you are taking money in exchange for pieces of your business. You are effectively selling a part of your business.

People who own shares in your company are just that - owners. That means they have a voice in your company and should potentially be involved in significant decisions related to the business. Some key rights for shareholders usually include: i) voting on significant issues ii) Ownership iii) the right to transfer ownership iv) dividends when they are given v) a right to inspect the finances / records vi) the right to sue the management / executives for wrongful acts.

If you self-fund then you are NOT selling equity to anyone but yourself which means you are keeping control of your company and you're not exposing yourself or the company to any of the 6 key shareholder rights just outlined.

Reduces Complexity:

Without partners and investors you can focus 100% on the business rather than needing to work with and manage your relationships with other owners. This allows you to concentrate on getting customers, making money and growth.

You Keep All Wealth Generated:

If you start and grow your company through just your own funding then when it's time to exit the business you keep all of the value that you've created with your business. If you have a desired financial outcome - let's say $10M (minus tax) then if you are the only owner, you'll reach that point in your business much sooner than if you have to share the value with other shareholders or partners. Example - If you and a shareholder each own 50% then your business needs to be worth at least $20M before you can exit and gain your desired $10M.

Exiting Is Simpler:

As the sole owner, if you receive an offer to sell the business at some point in the future, you can make the decision that is right for you at that time. You will not need to discuss or negotiate with others. That simplicity is true of all company decisions, not just whether or not it's time to sell.

Advantages of NOT Self-Funding

Self-Funding Alone Can Mean Reduced Resources

Getting investors has its downsides - someone new is involved in your business and you are giving up equity. Self-funding is far simpler - it's just you making the decision and what you say goes. Well, OK, what the customer says goes but you get my point.

If you self-fund you don't have to worry about other people being involved in decision making or in control. There is a lot to be said for self-funding.

However, unless you have a significant amount of personal resources, your ability to add funds to your business if you self-fund is restricted to your resources and the profits you can put back into the business and your gain customers. If in your business model resources have an impact on your ability to develop new products, penetrate new channels, market your product, sell your product and more than your available resources are a constraint on your business. Perhaps you don't agree but could you launch more products, get more customers, open new markets, sell more product with more resources?

If the answer is a firm YES then there may come a point in the life cycle of your company where you need to decide if it's the right time to consider alternative funding sources. If you are in a new market then you and your competitors are in a race to see who can gain the largest share of the marketplace.

As you and your business grow, it's possible to gain economies of scale. Whether it's because you can purchase larger quantities of your raw material at a greater discount or you can leverage your initial investment in fixed capital across larger numbers of products, the fact is as you grow you have the ability to become more efficient.

If you decide to only self-fund instead of increasing your access to capital through other funding sources, you are making a strategic decision in terms of your rate of growth. If you are in an increasingly competitive market, this funding decision will have an impact on whether you are an acquirer or an acquisition target - whether you are number 1, 2 or 4, 5 or 6. Maybe that doesn't matter to you and your culture, maybe being the largest isn't part of your or your company's DNA. If that's the case, that's cool. But if so, make the decision taking into consideration all of the strategic consequences of your decisions. Don't just make these decisions without being fully aware of their impact.

If you decide to forgo all funding sources except for self-funding - that can have an impact on your growth rate and the benefits your company could gain from a larger scale. If you are cool with that, great. If not, consider other funding sources in addition to self-funding. So be aware that limited resources Can Mean Slower Growth and Less Market Share (Important if you need a critical mass or economies of scale)

You Might Benefit From Adding More Experience and Smarts to the Business

If you are the sole decision maker in your business because you are the sole shareholder that can be appealing - no one to disagree with you so you can always be right, right? Well, not so fast. If you are the sole shareholder then no one can tell you that you're wrong. That is obviously a double edge sword. When I became the CEO of my first company that was the first time I'd ever been a CEO. Sure it was my business and I was passionate about bringing an amazing product to consumers but this was my first time making all the decisions. One thing that I knew immediately was that there was no way that every decision I would make would always be right. No one is 100% right all the time. In fact, you should probably be happy if more than 50% of your decisions are great or even good decisions.

For a company, especially a new company, making a whole string of bad decisions can have negative consequences.

My first response to this realization was to stop making decisions at all - to become frozen by the fear that a bad decision will bring down the company. It takes about an hour of that before you realize that no decision is a decision in itself. So how to cope?

Try to add to your talent pool - whether it's experienced employees, advisors, board members or all of the above.

Adding partners to the mix means you have the ability to add real experience to the business. It's true that you now may have someone on board who will not agree with you 100% of the time but who needs 'Yes' men. What you need is fast, efficient and best guess educated decision making that allows your business to make the right decisions and follow through on them in the market.

If you and your new shareholders disagree decide how decisions are made even though there is not 100% agreement - is there a time to reconsider the data, pros and cons? Is there a way for a third party to help break the disagreement? If you do take on another shareholder, make sure you discuss in advance who has the tie break or who is the ultimate decision maker.

The Risks Are All on Your Shoulders

If you are a sole owner then the risks are all on your shoulders. At least it feels that way. The realty is – if you have an LLC, then the risks are somewhat less than without limited liability. That's why it's critical to get a personal legal expert to give you the advice you need regarding the legal risks of starting and running your business.

CHAPTER FIVE: Friends and Family

SNAPSHOT

Friends and Family

Description:

Friend and family funding is getting the funding you need from close friends and family members. This is an extremely common way for young companies to get started. Just like the other forms of funding we discuss, you can offer family and friends the opportunity to lend you the money or sell them shares in your business. A loan will be a debt you'll usually need to repay and if you sell shares in your company, that is offering equity to your friends and family.

FOUNDER'S TIP:

Having worked with a number of entrepreneurs who go down the friends and family path, I recommend you treat it just as you would offering the opportunity to a regular investor. In other words, write an executive summary, perhaps a business plan and a presentation which takes them through the opportunity.

It's true they know you and that is a key aspect of their decision making but make sure they're clear about what they're investing in and what they'll get in return. I would always have a legal agreement which outlines what they get for the specific investment they make. This might sound odd or perhaps make you uncomfortable but there are a few important reasons why you should have a clear legal agreement with your first friend and family investors:

a) An agreement outlines the reality of the investment - not what people believe is the case and can later disagree about but the clear points

b) If and when you look for new investors - perhaps angels, accelerators or VC - they'll need to see the terms and conditions of the money you raised prior to their involvement. When money is raised without clear legal agreements, there is the potential for confusion, disagreement and even legal cases between the founder and initial investors. When there is the potential for disagreement, it would be considered a more risky deal and is often described as an unclean deal. Having the terms and conditions spelt out clearly in the appropriate legal agreement, even with family and friends, is the way to go.

The Investment Amount Sweet Spot:

This would depend on your family and friends. I've seen entrepreneurs raising different amounts from their personal network - most often between $10-$50K.

Stage of Company

Usually this funding source would be used for absolute startups and very early stage companies.

Types of Companies / Industries

Family and friend funding can be leveraged for all types of companies and industries. Given some industries require a significant investment for the startup costs - manufacturing being an example - there are some industries where friend and family are more common.

One consideration: even if your industry does require a significant investment to start the company, you could leverage family and friend funds to creatively undertake the customer research to prove the demand and that your concept would meet it - those family and friend funds could be what you need to build the case for more formal funding through angels or early stage VCs or perhaps to put the pitch together for customers or crowd funding.

Why Friends and Family?

One of the biggest questions investors have is 'can I trust this person to do what they say they're going to do?"

Trust is a key element for investors - they need to get to the point where they're comfortable risking their money on you and your business.

With family and friend - they've had years interacting with you and seeing your strengths and weaknesses. They know whether you are trustworthy, whether you'll get it done. As family and friends, they (hopefully) want the best for you so as well as trust, they'll have an emotional vested interest in seeing you achieve your goals.

What You Need to Pitch to Friends and Family:

I've seen entrepreneurs who ask their family and friends to invest with little preparation and walk away with a check. But I'd firmly recommend you treat this as an opportunity to practice a professional business-like pitch just as you would to professional investors. Create a kick ass executive summary, perhaps a business plan and pitch. Go through it like you would someone you don't know and treat it like a real business interaction.

Would you rather they made the decision because it's a smart business opportunity or because they have an emotional attachment to you?

By treating this as a real business proposal it gives them permission to ask difficult questions and say 'no' if they need to. If your opportunity is rejected, it will likely be because of a business reasons, which you can address and fix, rather than for some personal reason. It's also good practice for the next round of funding you may decide to do.

Their Criteria for Supporting Your Company:

You'll need to agree that with your friends and family - however, my recommendation is to clearly spell out and incorporate what the family and friends are investing in, what they'll get as the first investors and the real terms and conditions of making that investment. If you treat it like it's a business transaction it may seem a little odd but better that than it being brought up at every public holiday for the rest of your life - especially if the business is not successful.

Consider the friend or family investment being in the form of a loan, over an agreed time with a reasonable interest rate or offering them equity in your limited liability company. As part of the deal, agree the terms and how often and in what form you'll give them updates in the business.

Make sure you stick to those agreed terms.

What Do They Get for Their Commitment?

- If it's a loan then they should be getting the loan repaid according to the agreed terms and conditions
- If its shares in your company then what you give them will be outlined as part of the agreement you'll draft with a lawyer.

When They Want Their Investment Back

If you fund your startup through friends and family then agree with them the terms and conditions for their funds. Do yourself a favor and be crystal clear about these terms and conditions and consider having a legal agreement.

Why?

Although your favorite aunt may have decided to fund your business and be fine with a fuzzy outline of what she owns, when she gets paid back and your responsibilities to her - when companies increase in value and real money starts to be involved, it's important agreements are spelt out clearly.

Why?

Subsequent investors will want to know who owns shares in their potential investment and would like to see all contracts and documents which outline assets and liabilities. If you cannot show legal agreements which spell out who owns what, this could very well be a negative which makes them walk away from the deal?

Also, if Aunt Mabel sells her stake in your company or if she dies then everyone will be happier if the rights, responsibilities and ownership percentages she owned in your company are not open for dispute or disagreement.

When dealing with friend and family funding – consider getting a legal expert involved who will outline agreements and ensure everyone is clear about ownership, decision making, control and your responsibility to keep shareholders up to date on your company progress. Don't have some aspects in writing and other 'verbal' – they'll likely bite you in the ass later…

FOUNDER'S TIPS:

Friends and Family funding is going to Aunt Mabel, Uncle Ted and your immediate network and encouraging them to fund your business - either through a loan or by selling them equity (shares / units) in your company.

One of the biggest challenges with regular investors is getting them comfortable with the founder and the team. It takes time to develop trust with a stranger to the point where they'll sign a contract with you and transfer money through to your bank account. Obviously this happens every day between business owners and investors but it can take time.

With family and friends - you (and they) are a known entity. They already know if you have the drive and grit to take your company and do what it takes to go the distance. Your friends and family already know a huge amount about one of the key elements involved in your business - YOU. If they have expressed an interest in investing, now they just need to get comfortable with your business, the market, opportunity and those other key elements.

Whenever I've worked with other founders who are going out to friends and family for funding - I always recommend they treat it just like they would if they were going out to raise funds from a complete stranger and take them through the opportunity in exactly the same way. Ideally they'll make the decision on the merits of the complete business opportunity and not just because they've seen you in diapers.

Create a kick ass executive summary, a simple kick ass pitch and even a kick ass business plan. (Yes – I can help with each of those).

When you negotiate the deal, make sure you agree how you will keep them updated with your progress and make sure they understand exactly what they're getting for their investment - obviously include the agreed terms and conditions in a legal agreement written by a qualified legal adviser. No writing down the agreed deal on a paper napkin.

Why a legal agreement?

A couple of great reasons:

1) If your business is a multi-million dollar runaway door busting success, it's under these big money conditions that family members can fall out. If it's all spelt out clearly in a legal agreement - without any side conversations or agreements - then no one can feel like they're being screwed as soon as real money is involved. Now maybe you and Aunt Mabel have the best relationship in the world - if anything should happen to Aunt Mabel, you may find her assets being passed to a cousin or an executor. Having a clear, simple, clean cut legal agreement will save everyone heartache and reduce any confusion about what you and Aunt Mabel agreed.

2) Investors who may want to invest later will want to see all the agreements, contracts and legal documents you've signed since you started the company. Any deal which has people having an unclear ownership stake in the company put hair on the deal - in other words it increases the potential for disagreements and litigation. Not an attractive proposition if the new investors have a million or five tied up in the company that could be imploding because of a crappy deal not written down and agreed in a clean, clear cut and transparent way.

Why Friends and Family?

One of the biggest questions investors have is 'can I trust this person to do what they say they're going to do?"

Trust is a key element for investors - they need to get to the point where they're comfortable risking their money on you and your business.

With family and friend - they've had years interacting with you and seeing the strengths and weaknesses of your character. They know whether you are trust worthy, whether you'll preserver and get it done. As they're your family and friends, they (hopefully) want the best for you so as well as trust, they'll have an emotional vested interest in seeing you achieve your goals.

Pros:

- Good Deal Terms - lower interest rates
- Flexible Repayments
- Easy to get a decision

Cons:

- Potential for Meddling
- Family Squabbles

CHAPTER SIX: Customers

SNAPSHOT

Customers

Description:

To be a potential customer they should have a want or a need. If the potential customer recognizes they have a want or need, it's important enough for them to pay for a solution, they have the funds to purchase and they are willing to pay then these are the customers you should be trying to get on-board.

All of the above sounds obvious but so many entrepreneurs I've spent time with get so passionate about their ideas and their potential companies that they forget or ignore each of the above points.

If you are looking to start a company that is B2C - I.e. Business (you) to consumers, then you may want to take a look at the crowd funding chapter. This is one way to get customers to opt in and financially support the launch of your first product to market.

If you are looking to start a B2B - I.e. a business to business company, then consider the landscape of your industry and market and consider which potential customers not only have a strong desire to solve their want or need but have the funds to support a solution. If their problem or need is big enough, these customers could agree to become beta customers of your first product and cover some of the costs of doing so.

FOUNDER'S TIP:

How do you find out if they have a significant recognized need and if they're prepared to work with a team to solve it? Simple - ask them.

If your business intends to serve other businesses, connect with senior business people within your chosen industry and ask to chat with them, perhaps to interview them, about their industry. Many seasoned business people will be flattered and interested in chatting with founders of exciting new companies.

Example/FOUNDER'S TIP:

I worked with a team who were interested in building a software solution in a particular industry. They had a strong belief that a solution was required to address some significant inefficiencies in the industry so reached out to some of the largest companies in the space.

They pitched them on focusing 100% on the problem and building a solution to solve it. Three companies agreed to be beta customers and also agreed to take on some of the costs of building the solution on the agreement that they would a) be able to get the solution and b) that they would be able to have the solution for at least 12 months before any other customer.

Given the solution when through beta testing and improvements necessary to make it ready for prime time, this 12 month head start for the first three beta customers was ideal. This also gave the startup company the ability to tell the industry, after the first 12 months, that the solution had been built with input from industry leading companies who had also tried and tested the solution for at least a year.

In this case, this startup company was cash flow positive within 18 months of starting their company and they were able to achieve this without any investment from angels or venture capital (VCs). They only brought on-board VCs when it was strategically beneficial much later in their life cycle and were therefore able to call more of the shots in the VC funding negotiation.

The Investment Amount Sweet Spot:

The amount will depend on the costs of delivering your beta product or service to market and the perceived value of it. In the above example, they were able to secure circa $5M from strategic customers and their commitment was delivering a beta solution for testing.

Stage of Company

This customer funded approach can be used to start a company or perhaps explore a new product, market or geography. It is basically a technique of leveraging customers who recognize their strong need and have a strong desire to address it. Just as its possible for a startup to sign up customers in advance, it's also possible for a long establish company to reach out to potential customers in a new market and offer them the opportunity to support a beta solution both financially but also in terms of their creative input. It's great to have a key player in an industry involved as you then know you're building it to real need rather than guessed need and should help the company focus on the truly necessary features.

Types of Companies / Industries

Working with customers to support the development and launch can occur in just about any industry - the important factors are recognized need / want and the willingness and ability to support the development of a solution.

What You Need to Pitch To Customers:

A pitch deck that outlines the problem, the costs of that problem to the customer and an alternative scenario once the solution has been delivered. Do your best to quantify the time, money, market share and other costs involved in the current (less than ideal) situation and the potential improvement in time, money, market share etc. after you deliver the solution.

Your pitch should also outline the key elements of the solution including costs, time line and required resources the customer will need to commit. I'll be following up with a framework that will be useful for this strategic customer pitch so make sure to sign up for email updates.

Their Criteria for Supporting Your Company:

Each customer will have their own framework for evaluating your opportunity but they can basically be boiled down to:

1. How big a problem is this for us? (Time / Money / Growth / Market share etc.)
2. Is this a most pressing need right now or even in the top 3?
3. How much is this going to cost me?
4. What internal resources are required? (people's time being pulled away from other tasks)
5. Do these people have the skill set and experience to deliver a viable solution?

Answer these core questions to their satisfaction and you'll be making good progress to getting your first strategic customers.

What Do They Get for Their Commitment?

Most often the deals will include the following:

- Access to the solution

- The ability to input into and shape the solution that is best for them - (that's why it's important who you choose as your beta customers).

- Some degree of exclusivity for a certain period of time after the beta solution goes live

- The ability to work with you after the product goes live on new features and updates

When Do They Want Their Investment Back?

They want their investment back in the form of a solution within the promised time line.

Why Customers?

Customers with a strong want or need are looking for a solution. They are not necessarily looking to lend you money or take a slice of your company shares but if they have a problem that needs fixing then they could be convinced to support you if your new company will deliver the solution.

Startups can also gain support from strategic customers who see their stake almost as external research and development and a great way of keeping up on innovation in their industry. Larger corporations who recognize that innovation is a competitive advantage will often have a team or department with the express purpose of identifying young companies developing technologies which should be brought in-house - either for new product development or to enhance the existing business processes.

If you get customers on-board to help you fund and develop the beta product or service then you are not giving up shares in your company or taking on debt with them. Instead they are investing in a solution, and depending on the agreement, it could be more like paying for the solution in advance.

If you are able to strike an agreement along those lines then you are getting funds to start your business, launch your first product or service and the input from a key player in the industry.

Each of these things will help increase your company's credibility to other customers and viability as an investment opportunity to new investors.

All (?) you have to do is deliver the solution within the budget you have from the support of the beta customers.

Benefits of Customers:

- Letters of intent
- Beta customers - prepared to input into the design and development, specifications - beta customers are proof points for potential investors so having beta customers will help you secure investors or loans
- Full Paying Customers
- Recommendations
- Testimonials

If you don't have any customers - the short answer is - Go Get Some!

Whether you are trying to leverage passionate customers to fund your product development and beta testing or have decided to go fund your startup in another way - talking to customers is what will help you to become successful. I've started a few companies based on an idea I'm passionate about and a business plan but it wasn't until we sat down and really tried to understand our potential customers, that we were able to refine the concept to the point where it was valuable to the market.

Engaging passionate customers means you can refine your concept, understand the specific features that are really in demand and understand how to position (talk about / promote) your products to your customers so they strongly resonate to them and make them want to invest in your solution.

One way to get customers is to identify those who stand to gain the most from the launch of your product, service and company.

With that short list, get out there and ask them to spend some time with you so you can better understand what they need. You'll probably need to diffuse the conversation by being clear that you are not trying to 'sell them' but are just very interested in understanding what their needs are.

If they are not prepared to invest any time then either how you are communicating when your product will do for them is not appealing enough or they are NOT your target audience.

CHAPTER SEVEN: Crowd Funding

SNAPSHOT

Crowd Funding

Description:

Crowd funding is going out to your potential target customers and raising funds from them often in large numbers. There are various web based services which give founders the ability to raise money by offering their would-be customers the ability to commit to purchase a product or service when it's available.

One of the most well-known websites which helps founders leverage the online 'crowd' to raise money for new products and services is called Kickstarter. For entrepreneurs, Kickstarter allows you to propose a new project, product or service and take commitments from individuals who are promised different gifts based on the value of their commitment.

If you propose a kickstarter project, you decide how much you'll need to raise and within what time period. Your proposal will need to be compelling enough that potential customers will commit to pay when the product or service is available and ideally, promote your kickstarter campaign to others.

The Investment Amount Sweet Spot:

Today the average kickstarter amount raised is $21,224 and with a 37% success rate of all projects funded. That average is not exactly representative of the kinds of amounts that have been raised – in some cases 6, 7 and even 8 figures. To date over 250K projects have been launched on the Kickstarter platform.

Stage of Company

The different crowd funding services are targeted at individuals, teams and early or seed stage companies. In many cases the crowd source campaigns are just concepts or at prototype or beta stage.

Types of Companies / Industries

There are a number of web services offering these 'crowd funding' services - the most popular are outlined later in the chapter. In terms of the types of companies and industries they focus on, the most popular cover campaigns focused on technology, small business, film, photography and a whole range of other sectors including:

Animals / Art / Comic / Community / Dance / Design / Education / Environment / Fashion / Film / Food / Gaming / Health / Music / Photography / Politics / Religion / Small Business / Sports / Technology / Theater / Transmedia / Video / Web / Writing

Why Crowd Fund?

There are a number of benefits to crowd sourcing:

1) Getting Access to Passionate Potential Customers

You are engaging with your potential customers - if they are passionate enough about your proposed product or business and will financially commit to it in advance then you've proven there's real and passionate demand for your product.

2) Getting Access to Cash

Often one of the most challenging aspects of gaining investors is it's tough to prove your new business concept without the funds. It's a catch 22 situation. Before crowd funding, you needed access to some funds to be able to firmly prove you needed the funds. With crowd funding, they are marketplaces where you can line up customers before you have the funding and once you line up enough potential customers, they'll financially support your launch.

3) You Give Customers Products and Gifts Instead of Giving Investors Shares or Taking on Debt

When you raise money through most traditional means, you are usually either taking on debt or you are selling pieces (Shares / Units) in your company in exchange for the money. With crowd funding, the current approach is to offer a range of products or gifts in exchange for different levels of financial customer support.

For example - One inventor created a new kind of bee hive that would allow people to take the honey without disturbing the bees and without the other challenges such as using smoke etc. That new kind of bee hive went to a crowd funding site and asked potential customers to sign up. If they were prepared to pay $675 then they would get a new hive. If they committed lower amounts, they'd get key elements of the new hive design which would allow them to convert their existing hives to the new approach. Via the crowd funding site, they were able to get orders for more than $12M of new hives and their components - this was more than 17,000% larger than the amount they originally set out to raise.

You'll see in this last example that this inventor was able to raise $12M from potential customers and did not have to take on a loan or give away any of their company. Instead the inventor was required to take that $12M and go produce and ship those products to their new customers.

What You Need to Pitch on Crowdfunding Platforms:

Despite the fact that crowd funding is becoming a very popular way for founders and inventors to fund the start of their companies, crowd funding is not easy.

You need a few key elements - i) a strong pitch which really engages a passionate target audience and makes them want to purchase and ii) a way to target and engage with that audience both before, during and after your campaign.

I've known plenty of founders with great and worthy products who put their products onto one of the most popular crowd funding sites but then either get shy about promoting it to others or have not or do not have a marketing strategy in place to engage their audience. You'll need to create a strong, compelling pitch that clearly communicates the benefits of your proposed product or service fast.

Their Criteria for Supporting Your Campaign:

What Do They Get for Their Campaign Commitment?

Gifts, Perks or Rewards

- In most of the most popular crowd funding sites, the creators of the campaigns are offering potential customers a range of gifts based on the amount of money the customer is prepared to buy. It's basically getting customers who are willing to pay up front for a product or service and offering them different types of the product based on price.

FOUNDER'S TIP:

This is not only a great way to get money to go build a product but it's also a great way to get customer feedback on what products types they prefer and at what price. When you product is at concept stage you are guessing a) what features, benefits, the look and feel and more that the customer wants and is willing to purchase. With crowd funding you can take those concepts, assign a realistic price and let the crowd tell you which products they want. Once they do, it's up to you to go make those particular products and ship them to your campaign participants.

When Do They Want Their Investment Back?

When a potential customer makes a crowd funding commitment, they do so because you'll have told them what they get for their money and when you will deliver it. These deliverables are called perks or rewards. They don't usually get their investment back in the form of money but rather the gift or reward you've promised. In that regard crowd funding is more similar to working with customers than investors. You offer something, they decide if they want it and if so, they put their money up front and then, ideally, get what they chose at an agreed later date.

Estimate how long it will take, after the campaign successfully closes to create the perks or rewards and add a certain amount of extra time in case you run into any unforeseen challenges. When you make your crowd funding pitch you'll outline the different rewards they potential customer will receive for each commitment amount and the expected delivery date.

Once the campaign successfully closes, you'll need to take those raised funds and focus on creating and shipping those rewards. After delivering these rewards, if you've done your production, customer service and math right, you should have a) a list of happy customers prepared to give you a glowing testimonial b) made a profit and c) have proof that you have a viable business model. It's then up to you whether you take those things and go on to build a successful business around them.

Crowd funding is going out to your potential target customers and raising funds from them often in large numbers via the internet. There are various web based services which give founders the ability to raise money by offering their would be customers the ability to commit to purchase a product or service when it's available - these products or services are usually positioned as perks or rewards in exchange for the pre-commitment and funding.

Engage with New Customers

Crowd funding is a great way of engaging your would be customers. That is its primary benefit.

Providing your new product or service fits within one of the categories of the crowd funding web services and you engage your potential customers to the point where they support your campaign - then crowd funding is a great way to get your first set of customers and maybe the funding you need to get started.

It's true that there are break out companies who set out to raise a certain amount but end up tapping into a group of passionate potential customers who take that campaign to meteoric levels but crowd funding campaigns are not easy and the potential for crowd funding rock stardom are the exception rather than the rule.

So it's possible - through crowd funding to not only get your first set of customers and even be 'discovered' by your industry, the press and even investors. The stories of these successes do exist - but they are stories because they are rare even if they are compelling.

Product Development - Testing Your Market

Crowd funding gives you the ability to make different offers to your potential customers. In the Kickstarter market, when you create a campaigns you decide on a range of rewards and their values. You launch your campaign and ask people to commit to your campaign and to choose the reward they prefer. In this way not only do you potentially get the funding you need but you also are getting direct feedback from your customers on which reward they want overall and are prepared to open their wallets to buy. This is more powerful feedback than any form of focus group or customer survey - customers are only real when they actually decide to pay. Given this ability to create different offers (or rewards) if you have a few product types, consider offering the ones you believe will be most popular and see what your customers actually want.

FOUNDER'S TIP:

Make sure you can actually create and deliver the offers if you receive the funds you've requested - one of the most common challenges crowd funding folks face is underestimating the real cost of delivering the different rewards in the time frame they set. If you launch a campaign, factor in a safety margin as product development and delivery will normally cost more than you can estimate before you launch your product or service.

The Crowd Funding Results:

Kickstarter, one of the most popular crowd funding sites, had a 43% success rate in 2014 and a 37% success rate for most of 2015.

Pros and Cons of Crowd Funding

Pros

No Need to Give up Shares, Take on Debt or Give up Any Control

When you go through the crowd funding process through the current platforms of kickstarter, Indiegogo and others - those who financially support the campaigns do so either because they believe the campaign should be supported or because they want one of the rewards or gifts offered as part of the campaign. This is one of the few funding sources which does not require the founder to give up equity / shares in the company or oblige them to take on debt. The crowd funding model is basically encouraging would-be passionate customers to financially commit to the development of a product or service before it's available. As part of the crowd funding process the crowd funder outlines what gifts or rewards the customers will gain and the time line for the delivery of those gifts. When the deadline for the campaign, in most instances the would-be customers have the cost of their commitment deducted from their credit cards.

Early Validation

The main benefit of Crowd Funding is the early validation of a new concept, product or company. With the current crowd funding online systems it's possible to put a developed concept out to potential customers and see if they will financially support the project. Through crowd funding it's possible to get fast customer feedback before you go out and spend six or nine months or more raising money for a company before you've validated the concept. This early validation and ideally happy customers after the rewards are delivered gives the crowd funder the ability to take this success to angel or VC investors as proof of consumer demand, revenues and the founder and teams ability to deliver. Crowd funding is a great method of getting real world proof to investors and increase your companies valuation. You've moved your business from concept to revenues - that should have a positive impact on your valuation and your ability to raise additional funds.

Extended Network:

The current crowd funding marketplaces encourage participants to share the crowd funding campaign with people within their network. In the case of Kickstarter, the total campaign amount needs to be underwritten by supporters or the campaign is unsuccessful. This encourages would be customers not only to optimize their financial support but also to push details of the campaign throughout their own network to increase financial commitments. For the crowd funder, this means with this financial approach, you could access an extended network much more deeply and quickly than the more traditional approaches such as angel or VC investors.

Rinse and Repeat:

In some cases we're seeing companies who launch a successful crowd funding campaign returning to the crowd funding community to launch a second related product. In most cases if the company was able to get the first product lunch successfully funded and a whole bunch of happy customers, their second product launch, if related to the same target audience, can be even more popular than the first. Example - Remix. A company I recently backed on Kickstarter (Search Kickstarter).

Failure turns to Success:

If you launch a campaign through a crowd funding platform, position your new product or company, offer a range of rewards and you crash and burn - is it all over? Of course not.

What that failure has likely taught you is the way you've position the proposed new product does not resonate with your expected target consumers. It could also mean that your proposed rewards, at those price points, are not appealing to your target consumers.

Guess what?

You can do it again - you can change up your positioning, your rewards, their price points and you can even target other audiences through ads and other marketing techniques. If this new campaign gets funded, you've just gained some really powerful insights into how your proposed product should be positioned, priced and which target audience you should be engaging.

This is saving your months perhaps years of failure.

If you persevere and are successful the second, third or even fourth try, you now know the formula of target consumer, product, positioning and pricing which you'll need to deploy when you launch your product to market.

Cons of Crowd Funding:

Crowd Funding is not all roses and chocolates - although there are significant advantages, there are also so real challenges to take into consideration.

Time Sink: Running a Campaign is a Near Full Time Job:

When crowd funding first began it was possible to put a campaign together and get it funded with quite simple, if not compelling, campaign. As crowd funding becomes more popular the campaigns have a higher and higher production value. In other words, it becomes more difficult for a campaign to stand out, get noticed, get publicity and get funded.

Whereas it might have been possible to put a decent campaign together in an afternoon, campaigns are become complete product launches - the copy is well written, the supporting videos are very high quality and the supporting material is complete an rigorous. Most of the campaigns are also launched with marketing campaigns which engage their target audience over the entire life of the campaign.

Most of the successful campaigns have been put together by a team over a few weeks, if not months and even so, there are no guarantees that the campaign will be able to tap into the demand required to get the campaign funded. Launching a product via a crowd funding platform is a time sink and if the campaign is unsuccessful, it could have negative consequences if you then decide to engage potential investors.

You Need to Put Yourself Out There:

This is probably both a pro and a con. If you have a great new product concept and want the world to support your campaign then being shy about it is not an option. If you rely on the organic traffic from these crowd funding sites for the world to discover your concept – you've likely already failed and you don't even know it.

Those folks who launch and run successful crowd funding campaigns that I've interviewed ALL agree that they had a constant, thought through and heavily proactive marketing campaign supporting their campaign. To have a successful campaign and to raise the money you need to get your product live - you WILL need to tell friends, friends of friends, the local newspaper, the school alumni newsletter, perhaps your family and anyone else you are even remotely affiliated with. Start brainstorming those sources now. You will need to talk to as many people, asking them to forward your campaign on to others.

Do you have to promote your campaign?

Yes. Putting your campaign out there and trying the crossed fingers approach to marketing will likely get you exactly what you've put into marketing it, namely a big fat zero. If you go through all of this and still don't get your campaign funded, please don't quit. The fact you've tried means you are already 100 times more successful than those people who talk but never do. Even failing means you've gained insights into what you should (and should not) do next time and it could be the next time that is the attempt that is hugely successful. Laugh, shrug it off and try again.

You Make Very Little Money if you give consumers a significant deal:

If you want to attract a decent number of consumers to your campaign, you'll unlikely be able to include a significant profit margin into the total price of the rewards you offer. Most of the crowd funding platforms and the rewards offered tend to give early adopters are better price than the recommended retail price. A recent table that went through the crowd funding process on Kickstarter was offered through the platform at under $60. Yet after the crowd funding campaign was over, that same product was made available on Amazon.com for $349.

The Kickstarter early adopters got a great deal and the crowd funder gained very little profit - however they were able to take the proven product, the PR for it and the buzz created to launch it onto a major marketplace. The early adopters effectively funded the developers to iron out the product kinks and finish a great product but that first crowd funding product launch made them very little profit.

Difficult to Protect Your IP unless you've invested in IP Protection before the Crowd Funding:

Those who decide to crowd fund often do so because they have limited funds. When you put a campaign onto a crowd funding site, it's likely to be found by people internationally - that's a positive when it comes to funding but not so positive when it comes to companies going to these crowd funding platforms for interesting new product ideas. Yes you might have a provisional or full patent, you may even have a trademarks and more - however it's often tough and expensive to defend your intellectual property internationally. Having been through one of the largest intellectually property court cases in the United States - I can, hand on heart, tell you that it cost us close a decent seven figures to defend our intellectual property and more than two years of our lives going through the legal process. Most inventors and most entrepreneurs do not have that kind of money to defend their ideas.

It's worth mentioning that one of the largest aspects of that court case that worked in our favor was the fact we had a real product in the market being purchased by customers - yes we had patents, trademarks and copyright ownership of key aspects - but the fact we'd executed in the market and had long term customers was a strong positive for us in the court case. Consider how you protect your concepts - talk to an expert and then weigh up the need to get to market and start getting customers ASAP. Then make the right call for your business.

Current popular Crowd Funding platforms for inventors and startups:

- Kickstarter
- Indiegogo

CHAPTER EIGHT: Angel Investors

SNAPSHOT

Angel Investors

Description:

Individuals or groups of individuals who most usually invest in early stage companies most often before these companies have proven their business model in the marketplace.

The Investment Amount Sweet Spot:

- $5K - $100K

Stage of Company

Angel investors will typically fund very early stage entrepreneurs and the businesses. I've known angels put money into entrepreneurs who literally just have a business plan and that's it. So the angels can get involved very early in a company's life. One way to think about individual angel investors is they're most often the source you go to after you've fleshed the business idea out through self-funded, after you've chatted with your immediate friends and family and after you've tried or considered trying a crowd sourcing campaign. Angels will usually invest in young companies that are often considered some of the riskiest.

Types of Companies / Industries

Angel investors have been known to invest in pretty much every industry. A few data points pulled out of other studies suggest they typically invest in companies in industries that they are personally from or are very familiar with. When you think about it, that's logical as people need a degree of comfort before they'll let go of their money and what brings comfort? Understanding. So angel investors will be easier to get onboard if your business relates to an industry or space that the angels knows well.

FOUNDER'S TIP:

Whichever industry you are in, you'll be most likely to get an angel investor interested if they understand your space - that's one of the main reasons why entrepreneurs I've worked with will often find their angels by firs looking for relevant advisors for their new business. It's those people FROM the industry, when pitched to be advisors, who will occasionally step up to invest or will connect the entrepreneur with people within their network for funding.

Where to Find Them:

Individual Angels - Difficult as most individual angels do not 'advertise'. Individual angels can most often be found via your personal network and by that, think your real friends and family who you see face to face rather than your Facebook, Twitter or Instagram buddies. If you are not active within LinkedIn, now's the time as you'll need to mine your real personal network to access those who either may be angel investors or who may decide to become an angel investor to support your company.

Angel Networks - Some angel networks have websites, a regular meeting where they get together to assess opportunities and a process to follow to take part. I'll put some web addresses in the reference section but ultimately you'll need to do some digging in your neighborhood and closest city.

Super-Angels - similar to angel networks but often more informal, coming together to consider exciting opportunities when a member of their semi-informal network finds a new opportunity which they want potentially move forward with. In the case of Super-Angels, your friends and family, LinkedIn or through blogs, articles etc. is the way to go. Example - I leveraged my personal network to connect with Fabrice Grinder who has had $300M of exits from the companies he's backed. He is a super-angel and will bring his other wealthy friends into a deal when he finds a business which excites him and meets his criteria.

Angel Investor Marketplaces - There are various sites which have attempted to bring angel investors together around investment opportunities. However, as angel investors have typically invested in companies within their local geography, these virtual investor marketplaces have had varying degrees of success for entrepreneurs who are looking for angel investor funding.

What You Need to Pitch Them:

The short answer is differs by angel and angel type. Most what I'll call traditional angels will want to see a kick ass executive summary and if it really does kick ass then after they've read your executive summary, they'll want you to come in and pitch them. If the pitch excites them, they'll sometimes (although not always) want to see a kick ass business plan. That means you'll usually need a kick ass executive summary, a kick ass pitch deck and kick ass business plan. Of course you can go into the process without these things but if you're asked for them and don't have them, you'll either need to create them FAST or you'll need to admit you didn't bother creating them.

Although not every investor wants to see a business plan, I recommend entrepreneurs create one as it helps them think through the strategy, risks and gaps in their business…better you've identified these BEFORE speaking to potential investors rather than during an investment discussion. Consider your kick ass executive summary, pitch and business plan the tools you'll need to get the investor - you might be lucky without them but do you want to bank on luck?

When I went through the funding process, the first time took me almost a year, part of that time was figuring out the common questions investors asked, the best way to respond to them and during every meeting my pitch, executive summary and business plan evolved, got clearer and more focused.

Their Criteria for Investment:

Each angel investor has their own personal investment criteria. In some cases they've really thought through that criteria and it's a real checklist an investment will need to meet. In most cases it could be less rigorous. However when I've spoken with other angel investors, there are commons elements they'll describe.

They'll be focused on the strength of the founder, the team, the business model, the size of the market, the opportunity to scale the business, the competition, whether or not the business excites them and if they believe they can make a difference. Sure there are outliers of angel investors who want nothing more than to put their money in a range of businesses, step back and let the founders get on with it without their help or support - but most Angel I've talked with want to be a part of the company's story.

What Do They Get For Their Commitment?

- **Equity**
- **Preferred Stock -** A preferred stock is called this because the holders of this stock are preferred over common stock holders. In other words, if stock holders are to be paid back, the preferred stock holders are paid back before the common stockholders. The preferred stockholders are 'preferred' before others.
- **Convertible Notes -** Convertible notes can have many different characteristics so you'll need to chat through these instruments with an advisor. The basic concept though is it's a note which can be exchanged for common stock at an agreed discount during the next round of investment. *NOTE TO THE ENTREPRENEUR:* There are challenges for both angels and the investors in the next round - often due to the pricing of convertible notes. In many cases the angels are looking for a significant discount given the risks they've taken and the next round of investors often see this discount as unfair given what they are getting for their investment.

When They Want Their Investment Back

Most angels would be surprised if they get their money back and a return on their investment within 1-3 years. If that actually happened, they'd probably be overjoyed. The duration that would be on the outside of their comfort level would be much beyond 6-7 years. Most angel investors are thinking their investors will go through some kind of liquidity event (investor speak for an event which pays them back) within 4-5 years.

That event could be the company being acquired or going through an IPO. In either of these two cases, they would be able to potentially get their original investment paid back along with some additional amount of money (often called 'upside'). The upside will be determined by the difference in value between the shares when they purchased and the shares when they sold.

What are Angel Investors?

Go along to Wikipedia or dictionary.com and you'll find a nice clean cut and academic definition for an Angel Investor. It would be an easy job to cut and paste it over here but I'd rather include my definition based on my experiences.

So simply put - Angel investors are people just like you and me who have some disposable income and have decided to put it to work by investing in companies.

Nice and simple right?

But let me unpack elements of that sentence for you that are worth calling out.

Angel investors are people just like you and me.

Maybe at this point you're a little incredulous - angel investors have lots of cash right? That makes them special and different and motivated by making more cash right?

Wrong.

Angel investors put on their trousers, skirts or whatever they wear one leg at a time just like you and me. Sure they might have some money which they want to invest but they are driven by a range of motivations just like you are. Just because they are angel investors doesn't mean they are motivated by making lost more money. Some are sure...but most angels want to work with people they know, like and trust.

They usually want to get involved in companies they understand in some way - perhaps it's the customer you serve, the industry you are in, the product or service you create, your business - most angels will tend to invest in companies which are related in some way to what they, as individuals, understand and are excited about.

An Angel Investors Mental Checklist

When they look at investments, there's a mental checklist they'll go through (whether they know it or not) when considering an investment. This mental checklist is mine - meaning I created it to outline the conscious and unconscious questions investors consider when looking at an entrepreneur and their opportunity.

- Do I like this person? (You)
- Will this person be a pain in the ass to work with? (No time sinks allowed)
- Will I need to hold this persons hand? (#2 No time sinks allowed)
- Does this person get it or are they full of crap? (Investors have a BS detector - try not to set it off by talking crap. Fess up if you don't know something)
- Will this person get it done no matter what? (Do you have the grit to see it through?)
- Is this opportunity in a space I'm interested in? (Personally exciting space)
- Do I understand how this company is going to make money? (Is your business model clear?)
- Is this opportunity significant? (How big is the revenue potential?)
- Does this business have a shot at being a significant player in the market?
- Is the business scalable?

- Will they be able to execute on this idea without raising huge amounts of money later?

- Can I add value to this business and entrepreneur above and beyond the money?

- Do I like it? What does my gut tell me?

Angel investors can range in experience and complexity.

The Inexperienced Angel Investor:

Some angel investors have never invested in a business before, meet the founder, get excited by what they are trying to achieve and decide to invest some of their disposable income in exchange of shares or units in the company. These folks are inexperienced as angels who, for whatever reason, were captivated by the company they invest in. Perhaps they were introduced by friends or family members, perhaps the entrepreneur reached out to them because they have experience and a background in the industry the founder is attempting to penetrate and grown in. These one off angel investors are at one end of the spectrum.

The Traditional Angel Investor

Once upon a time you had lawyers and dentists putting their cash into various projects just to make a return on their cash. We can consider these the 'traditional angel investors'.

Benefits of Angel Investors:

Angel investors have the power to give a range of benefits to the entrepreneur - it's entirely up to you if you take any, some or all of them.

Money:

Of course they can give you some or all of the cash you need. Not all the cash you'll need forever but the cash you need right now...

Connections:

If the angels have experience in your industry, don't be shy about asking them to connect you with their network who can be helpful. Good angel investors should be motivated to help you as they now own part of the company. See if they can connect you with potential customers, employees, suppliers and when the time is right, new investors.

Advice and Experience

If the angels have experience then they can often be good sounding boards for challenging or strategic decisions you might have. They can be good advisors due to their experience generally, or because of their experience in the industry you're in. Also, because they're not involved in your business day to day, they'll not be as close to it as you, that can also be an advantage. In the beginning you'll probably be living your business 24/7 and won't have the distance you might need to make some decisions. Talking those through with someone - whether it's an advisor or an angel investor, can be helpful.

Credibility:

If you angel investor has analyzed your business and decided to risk their own money in your business it's a mark of approval. If they are well-known with experience in your industry - this enhances your credibility with potential advisors, customers and future investors.

There are a couple of ways to look at what you need to 'give' when raising funds for your new business through Angel Investors.

What Do They Get For Their Commitment?

If you take funding from an equity investors - such as an angel investor, venture capitalist and usually friends and family - then you are receiving their funding in exchange for a part of your company.

Let's go a little deeper into it.

If you allow angel investors or VCs to invest then most likely you'll 'sell' them equity in your business. In that instance they own a piece of your company. It's not debt, it's not a loan and you are not required to pay your investors their money back as if you had borrowed the money from a bank.

As these angels or VCs now own a piece of your business, they are now joint owners. In this case, if you sell the business at some later date, these investors will usually gain a percentage of the purchase price you received determined by the percentage of the company they purchased. If they bought 5% and you sell the company for $100M, then these investors, providing their shares are still worth 5% of the company, will receive 5% of this $100M I.e. $5M.

So the first thing you give equity investors when you take their funding is a small (or large) part of your company - just how much depends on your ability to negotiate.

What do Angel Investors Want?

Please remember that angel investors are all different. This is an important point. Too many entrepreneurs I've worked with go into these angel investor pitches and assume they know what the angel wants. Founders often assume the main motive is to make money. If it really were the main driver then pitching and closing angel investors would be easy.

Over time I've come to the realization that angel investors (or any investors for that matter...) have two sets of considerations.

1) The types of companies they want to invest in and
2) The types of entrepreneurs / teams they want to invest in

The type of companies they want to invest in will focus on questions about the industry, the company stage, the business model, the competition, the opportunity to scale, to dominate and many of the business questions that make the investment attractive or unattractive to them.

The types of entrepreneurs or teams they want to invest in is often less defined and concrete and touches on more touchy feely elements such as do I like this person, do I trust them, can they get it done, will this be fun, exciting, tiring, painful and questions along these lines.

Think about it.

Imagine you start your company, grow it and one day, you sell it for a gazillion dollars.

You think to yourself - "I know, I'll invest in a few startups and help some other entrepreneurs out…"

There's a big hurdle another entrepreneur will need to get you over - is this business going to be a winner.

They pitch you, you do some due diligence and make a decision that this really could be a winner.

Only trouble is the entrepreneur is boring as all hell, or looks like a slippery customer, or wants you to be their business Daddy….

Will you invest or pass on it?

And let's say you DO make a gazillion dollars selling your company, is making a million more worth lots of headaches? Probably not right….So why is it that most entrepreneurs think money is the prime motivator?

Money might be a good way to figure out the winners and the losers but I've known more angels motivated by working with cool entrepreneurs, or bringing cool products to market, or advising other younger entrepreneurs, staying fresh, making a difference…

So when you meet with your potential angel investors it's your job to figure out what is driving them. It might be money but it also might be working with cool entrepreneurs, having fun, changing the world, building an empire - either way money is rarely the prime or only driver. Figure out what the angel is looking for and decide if it's what you're also looking for.

What's that now?

Yes - if you are building your company to change the world, don't go into business with investors whose primary motivation is making loads of cash.

Not only do you need to figure out what the angels want that you're chatting with - you need to figure out if they want the same thing as you and you're team.

Although you might think NOT getting the money is the worst case scenario, it's not.

The short answer of what angels want is to invest in a company, an entrepreneur and team that will help them achieve their personal objectives. Those objectives can be making money, having fun, changing the world, building an empire, making them feel important as an advisor or ALL of the above - and more.

Your goal is to figure out what the investor's personal objectives are and make sure they line up with your own BEFORE doing any deals. Being blinded by the color of their money and figuring it out AFTER doing the deal is a HUGE mistake. Don't be afraid to walk away from a deal, just like there's a market for most products, if your opportunity deserves investment then, with persistence, you'll get the investment.

And Yes, it easy to write, and very very tough to live. In this case, I'm happy to be on this side of the page...

You need an opportunity which is investment ready. To prove that your business is ready for an investment, you need to be able to take angels through the key aspects of your business. The tried and tested way to do that is through the following tools:

- A Kick Ass Executive Summary
- A Kick Ass Pitch Deck
- A Kick Ass Business Plan

Some angels will want to see all of these, other investors may make a decision on the basis of a pitch deck and a 30 minute conversation. But just a pitch deck and a quick chat is less likely.

Each of these tools are used at different stages in the process of engaging an angel investor.

- The executive summary is most often used to GET the meeting.
- The pitch deck is used AT the meeting.
- The Business Plan is often something you leave behind or send after the meeting.

CHAPTER NINE: Venture Capital

SNAPSHOT

Venture Capital

Description:

Venture Capitalists (VCs) are individuals or teams who invest in companies. Companies which invest in established, older companies may call themselves VCs but a better term for them is private equity firms.

The VC description may sound similar to the angel investor description and the line between VCs and Super Angels is blurred. To help you decide if you should be approaching VCs or angels I'll take you through some of the 'usual' difference between the two.

VCs have traditionally invested in companies that are further along than those companies angels tend to invest in. Angel investors are usually investing their own money. VCs typically raise the money they invest from multiple sources, called limited partners and in doing so, create a fund. When they raise the money for these funds, they outline to their investors what their investment strategy. They describe what sectors, stage of company, investment processes they'll adopt - as part of those discussions, they'll discuss the target return they'll deliver with the fund. I.e. the rate of return and the time period they expect to gain this return for their investors.

The Investment Amount Sweet Spot:

VCs are not all the same. Meaning there are small VCs with less than a handful of partners who will focus on early stage companies. They could be comfortable and have made the decision to invest circa $500K. Their sweet spot could be making an initial investment of $500-$1M. However, those VCs which have significant funds, they're sweet spot may start at initial investments above $1M. There are also VC funds which won't get involved in an investment unless they can put in more than $3M.

If you are looking to get VC investments - that point is important. Decide what amount you are able to justify given the stage of your business and the amount you are looking to raise. Engage VCs that make investments in your sector and that size range. Don't try to pitch a small deal to a big established VC that is known to invest large amounts in more established companies. Those VCs who invest smaller amounts are often comfortable with earlier, less established companies. The VCs investing larger amounts are likely looking to invest in more established companies.

Stage of Company

Small VCs can focus on early stage companies but the majority of VCs will invest in companies that are later stage/ how can you determine what stage you're at? It comes down to what business milestones you've achieved. Also go take a look at the section on "Company stage: What Stage Are You At?"

Types of Companies / Industries

- Companies in the industry categories / sectors they focus on
- Companies in a space they want to invest in
- Companies at the stage they want to focus on I.e. early stage (complete)
- Founders and teams they've had success with before

FOUNDER'S TIP #1:

Most VC I've interviewed when asked what is the key driver when making an investment decision will say the founder and team.

FOUNDER'S TIP #2:

There are different opinions amongst VCs in terms of how they manage their portfolio of companies. In some cases VCs are comfortable investing in similar, perhaps competitive companies. Although overall many of the VCs I've discussed this with will try not to invest in companies which are competitive. When considering which VCs to reach out too - take a look at their portfolio on their website and see what types of companies they invest in. See if any of the companies are similar to yours in terms of business model, target customers, technologies etc. If they have a company in their portfolio which could be competitive, weigh that up before reaching out.

FOUNDER'S TIP #3:

Having gone through this process of evaluating the target VCs portfolio companies and having deciding which VCs to reach out too - consider reaching out to the founders of some of their portfolio companies to a) understand the VC better b) their selection hot buttons and c) any watch outs - also be great to have one of those founders give you a warm referral directly to the VC which will likely get you to the front of the line.

Most VCs have a comfort zone - they've got experience in certain industries and sectors and that's where they like to play. Your

Where to Find Them:

- Personal Network
- LinkedIn
- National Venture Capital Association

What You Need to Pitch Yourself:

VCs are often in even more demand for their time than angel investors. Given that most VCs will want to see a kick ass executive summary and if it's a potential fit, they'll want you to come in and pitch them. If the pitch excites them, they'll sometimes (although not always) want to see a kick ass business plan. That means you'll usually need a kick ass executive summary, a kick ass pitch deck and kick ass business plan. Of course you can go into the process without these things but if you're asked for them and don't have them, you'll either need to create them FAST or you'll need to admit you didn't bother creating them.

Although not every investor wants to see a business plan, I always recommend every entrepreneur goes through the process of creating one as it helps them think through the strategy, risks and potential gaps in their business...better you've identified these BEFORE speaking to potential investors rather than during a pitch discussion. Consider your kick ass executive summary, pitch and business plan the tools you'll need to get the investor - you might be luck without them but do you want to bank purely on luck?

When I went through the funding process, the first time took me almost a year, part of that time was figuring out the common questions investors asked, the best way to respond to them and during every meeting my pitch, executive summary and business plan evolved, got clearer and more focused.

What They Most Often Want for Their Investment:
- **Equity** – Shares or units in your company
- **Preferred Stock -** A preferred stock is called this because the holders of this stock are preferred over common stock holders. In other words, if stock holders are to be paid back, the preferred stock holders are paid back before the common stockholders. The preferred stockholders are 'preferred' before others.
- **Convertible Notes -** Convertible notes can have many different characteristics so you'll need to chat through these instruments with an advisor. The basic concept though is it's a note which can be exchanged for common stock at an agreed discount during the next round of investment.
- *NOTE TO THE ENTREPRENEUR:* There are sometimes challenges with convertible notes for both angels and the investors in the next round – often due to the pricing of convertible notes. In many cases the angels are looking for a significant discount given the risks they've taken and the next round of investors often see this discount as unfair given what they are getting (and giving) for their investment.

Their Criteria for Investment:

Venture Capitalists (VCs) are individuals or teams who invest in young companies.

Overview

VCs are most often a team of people who work together to invest funds they've raised from institutions and limited partners. When they raise those funds, they'll usually discuss with their investors, the strategy they'll have for gaining a good return for these funds. This strategy will touch on the sectors they'll focus on, the company stage and the expected time line for gaining the return for using these funds.

I talked with a VC in the last few days and he had just raised (often called 'closed') a $100M fund. In this case he'd raised that amount from one limited partner (LP) and is now looking for investment opportunities in the software space focused on big data, security and analytics.

Using this case, you can see that if you are a young company bringing an innovative software suite to market focused on data analytics for, let's say, the pharmaceutical industry then this VC and his team should definitely be a team you reach out to. However, if your business is focused on anything else. Don't waste your time or his by attempting to have a meeting.

Who Are VCs?

Their Background

The VCs I've met tend to fall into two camps - the VCs who went straight into VC straight out of business school or college and those who come to VC after starting, growing and having years of real world experience building businesses. I'm sure there are many exceptions of VCs who come to the career through other routes but these are the two I've seen most often.

Junior versus Senior VCs

As VCs, especially established VCs, have a significant volume of opportunities to consider - the more junior members of the VC team may be the first people you, as a new founder, will interact with. Although junior, these team members will be the ones wading through tens if not hundreds of applications and will, with luck and some time, be able to spot the real from the less attractive opportunities.

Areas of Focus and Interest

Areas of Focus

The senior VCs will each have their areas of focus and interest and have asked the team members responsible for the initial filtering of the application to look for opportunities of a particular type. If you go to a VCs website and look through the team profiles - they'll either state the kinds of companies they tend to invest in as their 'areas of focus' or they'll outline the companies they have invested in previously, or they'll outline the companies where they participate on their board.

Areas of Interest

Although a VC may have specific areas of focus, they may also have related areas which are of interest to them as potential areas for investment. As an example, a VC may have made a number of investments in science related fields and have an interest in find an investment in Nano technology although it's not an area they've invested in before. So when you are deciding which VCs to reach out to, make sure you shortlist those which invest in your industry and sector. But also consider engaging with VCs who invest in related industry and sector areas in case they're looking to expand their investments into your sector.

Assessment:

Given the volume of business plans, executive summaries, meetings and presentations established VCs gave to wade through, most VCs will implement internal processes for evaluating potential investment opportunities. These processes are put in place to allow them to make their best judgement on fit and opportunity in an efficient time frame. But just like publishing houses, VCs can have a significant sized 'slush pile' of documents to get through. Once they've gone through each executive summary, business plan and so on, they is usually a rigorous process of due diligence required before the VC will negotiate and invest in the opportunity.

FOUNDER'S TIP:

You should be looking for ways to short cut or expedite the process for your company. A few tips include - getting a warm referral directly to the VC through a friend or colleague. You'll be more likely to be able to get that first meeting if you have someone close to the VC recommend they meet with you.

If you don't know someone within the VC's network, go find someone - connect with a founder they've invested in, or sit on the board of, and reach out to the founder - ask them if you can chat with them about starting a building a business - you'll probably find they find the time to help a fellow founder. Ask them about getting funded, the challenges and stories - ask them about their current investors and if they've been helpful. If you get on well with them, consider asking them if they'd mind making an introduction for you to chat with their VCs.

Another way to speed up the process is to recognize that there IS a process.

VCs will tell you on their websites what their preferred application process is - if they do, follow it. If they don't, create a kick ass executive summary and get it in their hands - ideally via a CEO/founder within their portfolio or a business person sitting on a board with them. Ask them for a meeting. (See resources for help on creating your own kick ass executive summary)

You'll need to take a kick ass pitch deck to that meeting and have thought through the key gaps, challenges and needs for your business.

If you were to sit down with ten or a hundred VC you'd get different answers to what they want but there are significant overlaps to these answers.

What Do Venture Capitalists (VCs) Want?

Investment Return:

They want to invest in companies which will deliver a 2, 3, 4 or more times return on their investment. So if they invest $1M in your company, they'll be looking for the equity they own to be worth $2, $3, $4M or more and ideally liquid and paid back within 4-5 years. By paid back, that doesn't mean you need to pay them back but instead, that they'll be able to 'sell' the equity they gain when they invest in your company, for those amounts. The ability to turn that equity into cash is often called a 'liquidity event'. So a VC will be looking to turn their equity into cash within 4-5 years - sooner is good too but most VCs would prefer that they get the return on their investment inside of 7 years.

Companies in their Sectors:

Individual VCs and their VC firms will usually have sectors they would prefer to invest and work within. There are VCs focused on most industries and sectors. The fact is though that there are certain sectors with a significant quantity of VCs who really understand the space and are actively investing - an example of this is the technology sector. Likewise there are sectors which have not traditionally grown through VC involvement and today, those sectors may have less VCs.

Strong Founder and Team:

Most VCs will tell you that one of the main factors which will make them move forward or pass on an opportunity is the founder and the team. Important questions they'll have - can the founder and team take this business forward and drive it to a liquidity event with the desire time frame? Do they have the grit, determination, skills and experience to get it done? Notice I put experience last in that list - experience is important as is having 'done it before' but it's usually not the key driver. Other factors which are important considerations related to the founder and team is whether or not the VC will enjoy the experience work with this team.

Important Considerations:

As most VC's get their funds from investors, there are some important aspects you should keep in the back of your mind when pitching and negotiating with them.

They Are Investing a Fund:

This fund dynamic for VCs has a few consequences for entrepreneurs as they have made commitments to their own investors in terms of how they will invest this fund. For this reason:

VCs tend to invest in:

- **Specific industry categories**
  - VCs will focus on those industries where they typically have a depth of knowledge, insight and the potential for significant growth. Although VCs recognize a certain percentage of their investments will fail, by focusing on the industries where they have deep knowledge, they should (fingers crossed) be able to mitigate some of those failures.

- **Target companies above a certain size**
  - When VCs consider making an investment in a new company, founder and team, they usually spend a considerable amount of time going through the necessary analysis. That process of analysis is called due diligence. Due diligence is a time sink. Some VCs only make a handful of investments a year but could wade through hundreds of business plans, competitor and market data, industry journals and so on, to truly understand the landscape and opportunity. Early stage companies with low valuations are riskier than later stage companies and don't put enough of the VCs money to work. As a VC which has to go through

the due diligence process, they'll often prefer to focus on less risky (and de facto later stage) companies where they can put a decent amount of money to work.

- **Deal Investments above a certain size**
  - ○ VCs I've interviewed have said they'll not invest in companies unless they can initially invest more than $1m and often even larger amounts. It gets back to the time to go through due diligence. Their usual model is to place decent sized bets as they are not able to undertake due diligence on hundreds of companies. If you are looking for more than $1M and can truly justify such an investment then VCs could be worth exploring. For investments less than that, you may be better to focus on angels, super angels or VCs focused on earlier stage than most.

- **Deals that optimize their likelihood of a decent return**
  - ○ The first time I raised money from VCs it took close to a year, had many meetings with different VC firms and also picked the brains of business school classmates who were full time VCs. One point that came through was that VCs can have a preferred framework for deals. In some cases the VC will be looking to gain circa 30% of the shares in the company and have some oversight into how the company is managed - perhaps through a board seat. Understanding that VCs can have these loose deal frameworks is important when you're thinking through how much your business is currently worth and what you're prepared to give to investors who back your business. Why can VCs have these loose frameworks - the rationale I've been told is they understand the percentage will get reduced (often called 'diluted') when the next rounds are raised. If the VC invests and gets a decent percentage and some oversight, the return on the investment is more likely to deliver a decent return to their fund if the company gets acquired or goes through an IPO (often called 'exits').

What You Need to Pitch to VCs:

You need different tools to efficiently and effectively go through the VC assessment process. It's possible for you to go out tomorrow (or even today) and start the fund raising process from VCs with little more than an email. The reality is there is a tried and tested process and tried and tested tools that help founders and VCs go through that process efficiently. You can try to buck the system, to do it without much preparation but you are going out to raise $1M, $2M or more - do you really want to half ass it and hope to get lucky when that kind of money and potentially the life blood of your company and the vision you have for your future is at stake?

If your answer is yes, close this book down and go give it a shot. Good luck. Hasta la vista.

There are specific tools and reasons for them that you'll need to go through the funding process with VCs, as follows:

A Kick Ass Executive Summary:

VCs could receive 10, 15, 50 executive summaries daily. You need your executive summary to grab them by the throat so they sit up and beg to meet with you. That does not mean to print your executive summary on glittery paper or cool graphics so it's obnoxiously different.

This is not a circus clown resume moment, this is the possible start of a professional partnership

Instead of relying on formatting and crass printer techniques to stand out, your kick ass executive summary needs to cover the key elements the VC needs to make a decision to meet with you, quickly and powerfully.

Respect their time and get to the magic of what you do - fast.

Notice I've said 'to make the decision to meet with you' a few times.

Why?

Because that is the absolute, #1, primo task of the executive summary. To get the VC to say

> *"Hell, I want to meet with this founder / team / company – How soon can we get them in?"*

Don't try to make your executive summary do all the heavy lifting of the entire close. Your executive summary should not be used to close the deal, it's the introduction that wet's their appetite and makes them beg to meet with you. (Find out more)

Just reiterating that point one last time - it's not about how much information you can cram into your executive summary, it's about getting the right information, in a clear, clean and compelling way. If you've had to screw with the margins of your one or two page executive summary and reduce your font to 8pt then you haven't distilled down your key messages to where they need to be.

Can you write a three page executive summary and load it up with the kitchen sink? Sure you can, you can do whatever you want. You can also spend the next eighteen months eating Ramen noodles and wondering why the hell no investors are begging you to allow them the chance to invest in your world changing company.

> *Remember - It's not just what you say but also how you say it.*

A Kick Ass Pitch Deck:

If your kick ass executive summary has done its job, perhaps supported by being forwarded by someone the VC knows, likes and trusts then, providing you've targeted the right VCs, you should have a few meetings set up.

What do you need to take to that meeting?

The #1 tool you'll need is a pitch deck.

The likelihood of being able to 'close' the VC in just one meeting is slim to none at best. Sure, you may be Superman or Supergirl but don't put that kind of pressure on yourself or them. Just get them interested, excited and pass the airport test. (Google the Airport test if that is unfamiliar...)

Whether they know it or not, VCs go into these first meetings with a set mental framework, a set of questions that they'll run through as they meet with you for the first time.

Those questions relate to your opportunity - in terms of 'fit', 'market', 'opportunity size' and then will focus on you and your team specifically.

The main purpose of your first pitch deck is get the VC to want to meet with you again and to get into much more depth.

That's one of the reasons why I try to make that first pitch deck and meeting a brainstorming session about the business, opportunity and market. It's also why it's good to get into a discussion about the challenges and gaps you have today in your business.

What's that? I should talk about my company's weaknesses and gaps? Shouldn't I try to hide these?

99% of the VCs I've met are smart as hell, especially about business models, what it takes to make a successful business and the most common challenges. Don't be afraid to discuss the missing pieces of your business. The fact that you've thought them through, identified them and already have a plan to solve them shows business maturity. It's also a great sign for the VCs that you'll not try to BS them but are focused on doing what it takes to build the business - even to the point of admitting that you don't have all the answers.

Having the last 50% of your first meeting being constructive brainstorming session is a better result that you talking for all of it. Don't think 'sell' or 'pitch' - think 'discussion' about your business, market, customer and opportunity.

The Right Mindset

If you've decided you want to raise funds for your young company from VCs I'd like you to consider making a few mindset shifts from the norm. Now you may be the exception rather than the rule but most entrepreneurs suffer from a few mindset challenges. I've had these same beliefs myself, have worked with entrepreneurs and have chatted with way too many who have had one or more of these beliefs.

What are those mindset beliefs you'll need to change?

The belief that your business, you and your team are so freaking amazing that you'll be able to wing it, be half assed about it and still get funding in a month or two. Hell, you'll just send out a few emails, have a few coffee shop meetings and you'll have all the money you need.

Perhaps you have had the best company, product, idea or concept there has ever been. Maybe you have the startup All-star team and a network that puts Donald Trump to shame. It might be unimaginable for you to believe that the investors will not be tripping over themselves to throw nearly free money at you. You may have all of these things and more but do you not think every entrepreneur believes they too have a world changing opportunity the investors would be lucky to get?

Not trying to burst your bubble here and you may very well have the best VC opportunity in your back pocket. The truth is having that belief is necessary and should help you when the going gets tough. But even so, you'll be doing yourself and your team a favor if you learn how to best connect with and engage with the VCs.

There is a recognized set of tools and a relatively standard process and by recognizing those facts, you can present your great opportunity in a way which makes it easy for the VCs to see the true strengths of your business opportunity.

The first time I raised VC money it took close to a year and in retrospect, a significant amount of that time was due to the fact that I was learning how to take a VC through my opportunity and needed to move my business forward. I don't want you to waste months like I did.

BAD: When you go looking for VC investors you think 'Sell' and 'Pitch' rather than 'Discussion and Brainstorm"

One of the best pieces of advice I've ever received is people do not like to be sold to but *they do like to buy.*

Instead of going into your first meeting with a VC thinking about needing to impress them, to wow them with your opportunity, to sell them on why this is the best they've ever seen, you might want to think of it as an opportunity to discuss your business, your market and all the facets of your opportunity with a smart business person and get valuable feedback.

Sure you might want them to invest, you certainly want the money they can offer you, but I guarantee if you go into that meeting looking to understand what they see as your strengths and weaknesses and to see if they have valuable suggestions - it will be a substantive and positive meeting.

If you walk into this meeting determined to 'sell' and 'talk them into investing' - you'll be doing most of the talking and not too much of the listening. The more you can get that mix to 50/50, the better the meeting will be and the more likely you'll get a follow up meeting IF the deal is interesting and relevant to the VC. No amount of fast talking can make them invest in a space that's not interesting to them, in a concept that's too early for their fund or in a company that's still half baked. Do yourself a favor and try to spend as much of the time having them give you free consulting - if you are targeting your VCs correctly, they see lots of companies in your space and can probably give you some good, tangible insights that could really help your business.

The Money Becomes More Important than Finding the Ideal Investor:

As you go through the process of raising money from VCs there may come a point where you really want the funding to be over and all you can think about is having that raised money in your company's bank account. Most entrepreneurs don't want to spend all their time raising money and would rather be out there building their business. Please try to remember that you need to get the absolute right investors for you and your business. It's totally understandable.

But try to remember that getting an investor is not just a financial transaction where when done, ignoring your investors, you go on to build your business. Taking on an investor is taking on a partner.

If that partner does not have the same goals, ways of working or ethical framework taking that person's money could be the worst thing you could have ever done to your business and your own sanity. Investors will take different degrees of involvement in the companies they invest - could be that they'll be available to help when ask or perhaps they'll want a weekly or monthly update. Make sure you and your potential investors understand this degree of involvement before doing the deal.

Due Diligence

Due diligence is the term most investors use to describe the process they take their potential investment companies through before offering them a term sheet and doing the deal. Due diligence will focus on the company, market, the founders, team, existing customers, the competitive landscape and other key aspects the impact the business they're considering funding.

This data gathering and analysis is the due diligence process.

When it comes to due diligence there are two vitally important recommendations:

1) Understand what the due diligence process is likely to be before engaging investors.

The more information you can provide as early as possible in the process, the more expedited the process can be. Having this data won't stop the need for due diligence but it can help speed up the process and get the deal done faster. The faster the deal, the faster you can focus on building your business, gaining customers and revenues rather than focusing on getting investors onboard. Getting investors is a process which requires you to evaluate your business more strategically. This is useful to help you fundamentally understand your business, the challenges you're likely to encounter and begin to develop tactics and strategies to resolve them. Further, by understanding the due diligence process in advance, it means you're more likely to go through that process successfully and arrive at a point where the investors are ready and comfortable to make the investment and become partners in your company.

2) Make sure you do your own due diligence of the potential investors.

This second recommendation can be where many entrepreneurs drop the ball.

Many entrepreneurs get focused on getting the money they need – getting the cash and at what valuation become the two absolute areas of focus. So many times entrepreneurs get caught up on whether or not they're going to get funded. Once they start to get traction with investors, they'll switch their focus to what 'deal' can they get i.e. how much of the company do they need to 'give up' to raise the money they're looking to close. Both of these points are important but having been a founder who has gained investors multiple times, WHO invests should be the first priority - even above the valuation.

When discussing WHO invests, some entrepreneurs are concerned about the brand of the investors who are willing to sign up as investors. Almost like the popularity or name of the investors gives them some inherent legitimacy or kudos - something akin to getting a degree from an Ivy League college versus a college that might, for whatever reason, be a better personal fit. It's absolutely true that there are some VC 'brands' that have invested in some phenomenal companies and if they invest in your company then you are part of a prestigious portfolio of invested companies….but what are you looking for from an investor?

Make sure you've figured that out for your business…

Once the money is in the bank, what else do you want your investors to do?

Perhaps you want them to disappear and let you get on with it?

Perhaps you want them to network on your behalf and get you access to customers, other investors, industry leaders and more?

Whatever your goals and desires for your investors - make sure you do your due diligence and not only will the ultimate investors you choose help you in the way you need and desire, but also that they have the same goals and you and your team for you and your business.

That you'll have the money in the bank from an investors is a given once you are ready for investment providing you go through the process properly - expect that and get beyond it, now be clear about what your investors need to do beyond the money and what are their aspirations for you and your business. Make sure these aspirations are the same as yours and if not, I recommend you move on and find some other investor who is on the same page as you and your team.

CHAPTER TEN: Accelerators

SNAPSHOT

Accelerators

Description:

Accelerators are a relatively recent innovation in the startup funding world.

Accelerators offer capital and mentorship in exchange for small amounts of equity (shares/units) in young companies. The model is evolving but in many cases accelerators will have the companies they support work onsite for a certain length of time to help get the company started and growing. In some cases they have a class methodology where they'll bring in a fixed number of young companies - will give them capital and will work with them day to day until they 'graduate' from the accelerator. The accelerators will require equity in their companies in exchange, may also offer their graduating companies the ability to take additional capital, perhaps in the form of a note, and may want to participate in the first round of external funding (Series A).

The Investment Amount Sweet Spot:

Accelerators have different 'deals' but the range is typically from $10K-$50K but most being on the lower end of that range.

Stage of Company

Startup; early stage; pre-series A

Types of Companies / Industries

There are accelerators in many industries/sectors. There are quite a few in technology, software, hardware, mobile, web development, clean-tech, biotech and others - plus most recently accelerators beginning in food innovation and to support those startups begun by minorities and women founders.

Why Join an Accelerator?

Accelerators are not just about funding. As the initial investment is often in the $10-$25K range, funding is not the key driver. Many companies who join accelerators do so for a few reasons such as to gain a mentor and a team supporting the startup at conception and during initial growth. In addition, many accelerators bring together a number of startups as a cohort and they go through the development process together, supporting and encouraging each other as they move through product development, launch, customer acquisition, strategic partnerships and potentially through to series A funding.

What You Need to Pitch Yourself:

Each accelerator has its own process of application. If you're interested in applying to an accelerator, make sure that you go to their website and follow step-by-step their specific application process. In terms of what you need to apply to an accelerator? A game that differs by accelerator. However, in most cases, having a fleshed out business concept, a core team, and some initial customer feedback, are good first steps.

Their Criteria for Investment:

Having been involved in judging applicants for a well-established accelerator, it is both an art and a science. Applicants are considered across multiple dimensions. The founder and the team, the concept, the initial traction, the uniqueness of the idea, are just some of the considerations when examining accelerator applicants and deciding if they should go into the next step of the process.

What Do They Get for Their Investment?

Each accelerator has its own approach to how they invest in their accelerator participants. In some cases they give a small amount of money say $10-$15K to cover expenses during the participation in the accelerator. In most cases this investment of money and time by the accelerator is in exchange for a certain amount of equity. In most cases, the companies that go through their accelerator program are offered a larger amount of money in exchange for a larger percentage of equity. This larger investment usually ranges from $50K-$100K or more.

When They Want Your Investment Back

As its equity in the company, the expectation is they'll get their investment back when there is some kind of liquidity event such as the company being acquired or going through an IPO. In other words, accelerators have a longer term horizon expecting to gain back a return in years.

CHAPTER ELEVEN: Loans

SNAPSHOT

Loans

Description:

Raising money through loans is getting money by taking on debt. In other words, when you take a loan, you are required to pay back that amount, usually within a fixed time and with an additional amount on top of the initial sum, often called 'interest'. Loans are different than gaining funds from most of the other sources we discuss because loans are not purchasing shares or equity in your company but are, instead, lending you the money for your company and are expecting the company to pay them back with interest. Most of the other forms of funding in this book are not debt and do not require repayment within a certain time.

There are various sources of loans and some sources have loan products and evaluation processes focused on young companies and small businesses.

Sources:

Banks, credit unions, and community banks.

The Investment Amount Sweet Spot:

Small business loans can range from micro loans of around $5K and increase to larger amounts up to around $350K. As you apply for larger amounts, the guarantees you'll need to provide will usually increase. In some cases those guarantees can be offering assets to the lenders if the loans are not paid back. Another method is to have another person offer an asset if the loan is not repaid. In the latter case, the 3rd party is acting as a guarantor of the loan in case you default (i.e. don't repay the loan with the agreed schedule of payments.)

FOUNDER'S TIP:

Banks can be more risk averse than other sources of funding. Also, as the loan amounts and interest rates make small business loans a relatively small revenue opportunity for banks, you'll typically find that the larger banks are often less interested in lending small businesses the money they need. If you decide to get a small business loan, you may want to focus on the smaller banks, the community banks and credit unions. Also if you have a long term relationship with a bank from a personal perspective, that relationship and history can be leveraged to gain a small business loan.

Stage of Company

Loans from banks and similar institutions are typically made to companies that already have revenues rather than to entrepreneurs who are looking for funds to start their business.

Often one of the easiest ways to get a loan for a business is via a type of loan called a line of credit. It's still important to understand that your business will usually have to have been in operation for at least two years before you'll be able to get a line of credit from most banks.

A line of credit is where the bank is allowing you to borrow money on credit, when you need it. This type of loan is most often used for day to day activities of the company. Loans in the form of lines of credit can be unsecured I.e. you do not need to put up an asset to guarantee you'll pay the loan back. Lines of credit can be useful in that they are flexible and you do not pay interest until you actually borrow the money. So as an example - you may agree that you have a line of credit up to $10K. If you spend $2K in a month on your business, you'll only be paying interest on the $2K rather than the amount you are allowed to borrow. Also, the rate of interest that you pay for lines of credit will often change to stay in line with the cost of borrowing money (often called the 'prime').

Types of Companies / Industries

Why Get A Loan?

As mentioned above, loans are debt rather than equity. What this means is the lending company is not taking shares in your company. You will continue to own all shares in your company until you either get an investor or give equity to others. So taking on debt can be one way of maintaining control and not giving up any decision making or ownership to others.

Another advantage of debt is you know exactly how much you own, the interest you'll need to pay is clear cut and you have a fixed time to repay the debt. From a cash flow and management perspective, there should be no surprises providing you keep to the agreed repayment amounts and times.

What You Need to Get a Loan:

You'll often need to show:

- Your personal and business credit history

- Personal and business financial statements

- Projected financial statements including cash flow projections for at least a year

- Strong, detailed (kick ass) business plan

- Personal guaranties from all principal owners of the business

Their Core Criteria for Investment:

- Ability to repay the loan according to agreed payment plan

- Ability to pay the agreed interest rate

- Likelihood of default

- Availability of security or guarantee

SBA Loans

Description:

Some banks and similar institutions are able to make loans on behalf of the Small Business Administration (SBA). The SBA is a department of the United States Government focused on helping small businesses. (A description and contacts for the SBA is included in the resources section.)

SBA loans are offered via banks - there are three main types of loans based on the amount and purpose required for the funds. Banks and the SBA suggest it's easier to get an SBA backed loan than a regular business loan from a bank as the SBA are guaranteeing your payments. I.e. if you don't pay it all back, the SBA will pay the banks back for your default.

Benefits of SBA loans are stated to be lower rates of interest, longer periods to pay back the loan (up to 7 years) and it's easier to qualify for an SBA loan versus a regular loan.

NOTE: Having discussed SBA loans with representatives of the SBA and the banks that administer them, I've been repeatedly told if you don't or can't qualify for a regular business loan from a bank, then you'll probably not be able to qualify for an SBA backed loan as the banks administer the process of evaluation and decide who qualifies for a loan, even those backed by the SBA.

SBA Loan Products:

Currently there are three main types of loans offered by the SBA and via banks. In other words, banks administer the evaluation process, the closing of the loan agreements and the ongoing administration of these loans on behalf of the SBA.

SBA Express:

Lending Value Range:

The SBA product is for loans between $25K and $350K

Purpose:

- Purchasing inventory, equipment and / or vehicles
- Working capital I.e. the cash you need to run the business day to day

Lending Period:

- Up to seven years; the first year can be via a revolving line of credit with the balance and interest amortized (spread) across the remaining six years.

SBA 7A:

Lending Value Range:

The SBA product is for loans between $350K and $3.5M

Purpose:

- Purchasing businesses

- Expand a business
- Working capital
- Purchase equipment or inventory
- Purchasing real estate for your business
- Pay off debt

Lending Period:
- Seven years for working capital
- Ten years for equipment / inventory / buying a business
- Twenty five years for purchasing real estate

SBA 504:

Lending Value Range:
- The SBA product is for loans between $350K and there is no maximum

Purpose:
- Purchasing real estate for your business
- Construction and renovation

Lending Period:
- Up to two years for interim construction period
- Seven to ten years on equipment
- Ten to twenty years on real estate

SBA Loan Pros/Cons:
- Longer maturity than conventional loan.
    - In other words, you have longer to pay back the loan versus regular loans from a bank or similar type of institution.
- Lower down payments on fixed assets.
    - If you are wanting the loan to purchase a fixed asset then you won't need to put as much down to be able to get the loan and purchase the asset. (Assets are called 'fixed' if it's tougher for them to be converted into cash - so property, plants and equipment are often considered fixed assets as they are assets less liquid than cash).
- Easier qualification than a conventional loan

○ The SBA believes it's easier to get an SBA loan from a bank than a regular loan. There are different opinions about whether that's generally the case.

The specific pros and cons of adding debt to your balance sheet via a loan will depend on where you are based. You'll need to check on where you are setting up your company - however, some of the common pros and cons of a company taking on a loan include:

Pros of Loans:

You keep control of your company.

A debt does not mean selling shares in your company and a bank will not tell you how to run your company. With debt, your responsibility is to repay the loan with an agreed additional interest rate, within an agreed timeframe. This is in contrast to taking on investors who will gain some percentage of you company, have a voice in how you run your business and at a minimum, will expect regular updates.

Tax Deduction:

In some countries, the amount a company borrows, called the principal and the interest rate payments can be deducted from your company's taxes.

Historically Low Interest Rates:

Combine a tax deduction with low interest rates and a modest inflation rate then the cost of borrowing money is lower than it's been in quite some time. In other words, if your company takes out a loan the amount you'll need to pay back above the amount you borrow will be quite small versus previous years.

Obviously those points depend on when you are reading this and whether you can deduct the interest payments and the principal from your company taxes. As always, make sure you get specific individual advice from an expert.

Cons of Loans:

Business is Unpredictable

Your need for cash and your monthly revenues will fluctuate however your loan repayment will not. Whatever happens in your business, your company will need to repay the agreed monthly amount on the agreed specific date, no matter what. The last thing you want is to default on a loan, especially if you or someone close to you has guaranteed that loan with an asset such as a home or similar.

You Need to Pay It Back:

With a loan you are paying back the loan and the agreed interest regularly and until it's completely paid. In contrast, when you get an investor, they are not giving you a loan but instead they are buying equity (shares / units) in your company. You are not obliged to pay the amount they invest back within a specific time period with a specific payment plan. Why? Because they now own a piece of your company, they bought it. They expect to get their money back and then some, when you either sell your company or its shares are purchased in a public market.

Time to Revenue:

Most startups take some time to make revenues and become cash flow positive. Debt funding doesn't care that it might take you months or more to make revenue - they've agreed a repayment plan with you and you'll need to stick to it. Taking on debt early on in the life of your company, before predictable revenues is risky. Always make sure you can pay the debt back and keep to the agreed repayment schedule.

You Need Predictable Revenues:

The short answer is - before taking on debt, you really need to make sure you have predictable revenue. If you have a small number of customers and if you'll miss your loan repayment if one of them pay you late, I would not take on debt under those circumstances. However, if you have a number of paying customers, paying you consistently and predictably so you can more than cover your loan repayment - why the heck do you need a loan?

CHAPTER TWELVE: Strategic Partnerships

SNAPSHOT

Strategic Partners

Description:

Strategic partners are companies in your industry that you can partner with to deliver a product or service to your joint market. Strategic partners are different from customers because you are not selling them a beta product or service but are instead, working with them, to deliver that product or service to a 3rd party.

For example - there are a number of consulting companies which work with large corporations. Those consulting companies may want to bring a solution to their clients but may not have the expertise in house. In this case the consulting company can recruit new staff to develop the solution, can outsource the solution to another company or instead, build a partnership with a company with the expertise they lack. In this case, the last option, partnering may be preferred as it offers a longer term solution and shares the risk of delivering a quality product across both partnering organizations.

FOUNDER'S TIP:

Where I've seen this funding approach work best is when the more establish strategic partner works with the junior partner to develop a new solution which they then go 'pitch' to their existing customer base. In that case there is not a significant cost to pitch a new product or solution. If the customers bite and want the product or service offered, the more established partner can either fund the initial development after signing up those interested customers, or have the interested partners pay for this initial development. Most potential partners will be unlikely to fund a new company and new solution until they've had it strongly validated by a number of their potential customers.

Example/FOUNDER'S TIP:

Companies who gave funding from strategic partners will often need to be careful about the ownership of the intellectual property jointly developed. Make sure you take legal advice from a legal expert before moving forward with a partnering agreement, especially in the area of IP ownership. You don't want to be locked into only being able to sell the products and services you develop through the partnership and further, you also do not necessarily want to owe the strategic partner revenues from all product and service sales.

The Investment Amount Sweet Spot:

Investments by strategic partners will usually be focused on a specific deliverable - whether that's a product or solution you may be developing together.

Stage of Company

This type of funding can occur at most company stages.

Types of Companies / Industries

There is no reason why this funding approach can't work in most industries. I've seen it in a number of industries.

Why Strategic Partners?

What You Need to Pitch To Strategic Partners:

A strong pitch, a number of customers that need a solution they're prepared to pay for and a strong story that both companies together can deliver this solution. Most products and services cannot be delivered in isolation - for example, most product companies require marketplaces, retailers, delivery agents, customer support and so on. If you want to start and grow a company, consider what elements your business will need successfully deliver the product or service to paying customers and consider which companies could partner and gain from your new business.

Their Criteria for Supporting Your Company:

Will differ by deal, industry and company but the proposition that company A + company B are complimentary and together can gain consistent and growing revenues from customers. Then you'll need to be able to prove it and then work together so there is value created for both companies and your customers.

What Do They Get for Their Commitment?

- A solution or product which delivers new customers and revenues.
- Perhaps a small amount of equity (shares / units) in your company
- Other elements specific to your deal

When Do They Want Their Investment Back?

This depends on the deal. The motive is more likely to be the ability to offer their customers a new solution or to be able to penetrate a new market or product category.

What is Strategic Partnership Funding?

This is when you partner with an established company within your industry and where you work together to bring a solution to market. In some cases strategic partnerships are successful because both companies have complementary strengths and together are able to bring a solution to market. Perhaps the more established company has existing channels to market, a sales team, buyer relationships and perhaps your company has some new products or a new technology. If there is a case for working together, it's possible you can make the case to potential strategic partners to support you in your efforts to develop your new product or service.

In this situation, the joint solution can mean revenues for both you and the strategic partner. If there is a case for partnering, they may request for some degree of exclusivity in the relationship. If so, consider agreeing common sense rules of engagement such as the customer being a key decision maker in the partnership - so if the customer agrees to purchase a joint solution then this partnership works for all concerned. However, if the customer insists on using your solution in combination with a different company, arguably the customer should be the ultimate decision maker.

CHAPTER THIRTEEN: Grants

SNAPSHOT

Grants

What are grants?

Grants are amounts of money, made available for specific purposes. Grants are often provided by government departments or, organizations, and companies.

Given that grants are made available for specific purposes, the application processes are often time-consuming, complex and require a significant amount of supporting evidence. After submitting your grant application it can take months or longer before you get a response. In most cases, grants are not successful. Given the amount of time and effort required to make grant applications. My personal recommendation would be that you consider investing that time and effort on an alternative funding method. It can literally take months, and the chances of a successful result are very slim.

Pros and cons.

Pros:

1. Grants can seem like free money

Grant money is made available without requiring a repayment. Also grant monies received without requiring equity to be given in the company. This makes grant money seem like free money. However given the amount of time required to prepare for and apply for grants, grants are certainly not free. There is a significant opportunity cost, and you should consider if the time would be better spent talking with potential investors, or customers.

Cons:

1. Complex, Time-consuming, Likelihood of Success Very Low.

Enough said.

CHAPTER FOURTEEN: Resources

Rather than weigh you down and give you hundreds of resources to pursue in multiple directions, I've chosen the few which can have the quickest and perhaps best impact. There will be big gaps so let me know if there are resources you need and I'll see what I can do about qualifying and providing. (Andrew (at) andrewive.com – yes, this is my real email so please – keep it spam free and clean ;))

Recommended Books

The Lean Startup; Eric Ries: All about creating the lean startup and business.

Influence, the Psychology of Persuasion, Robert Cialdini: Get inside the heads of your new customers and position your product to optimize growth

Selling the Invisible, Harry Beckwith: Great book on how to get your marketing right for any new or existing product.

Rework; Jason Fried et al: An alternative approach to this whole fund raising thing. Worth considering as an alternative approach.

Get Your First Investor Meeting, Andrew D. Ive: Focused on putting together a kick ass executive summary so you can get that first meeting with Angel investors or Venture Capitalists.

Helpful Websites:

Http://www.AndrewIve.com

This is my personal website focused on entrepreneurial challenges, insights and questions. It's also a great way to get into contact if you have suggestions, questions or need help.

Http://www.TheFundingGuru.com

This is our website focused on tools, courses, webinars, podcasts and blog focused on all aspects of starting, launching and growing your business. Also another good way to connect if you have a business request.

Online Courses via Udemy.com:

Funding Academy Express: How to Get Your Ideal Investor; Andrew D. Ive

Handling Investor Objections; Andrew D. Ive

How to Find Your Startup Investor; Andrew D. Ive

Angel Investor Supercharger – Speed up Your Fund Raising; Andrew D. Ive

Funding Related Websites:

Angels

Multiples angel networks can be found via Google however I've heard and experienced good things about the following:

AngelList: An online service bringing together angels and startups. Consider that many angels like to invest in companies that are reasonably close physically. I.e. it may be tougher to close an angel which lives and works on the other side of the world.

Venture Capital

National Venture Capital Association: The hub for the Venture Capital industry in the United States. Let me know if you'd like the same types of sites globally. A good place to start your research.

Crowd Funding

Kickstarter: A crowd funding platform that spans multiple categories and industries.

Indiegogo: A rival crowd funding platform to Kickstarter covering multiple categories and markets. Good traction with consumers so expect both traffic but also competition. Figure out how to stand out from the crowd.

Krowdster: Great tools for perhaps the most important part of a successful Crowd Funding campaign – engaging your market, getting press and the support of key influencers.

Loan Related:

Small Business Administration: Government department focused on small business. May have loans or links to loan details on their website. A range of resources and support of varying degrees of helpfulness available from the SBA.

CHAPTER FIFTEEN: What's Next?

What's Next?

Your next step is to decide which funding approach is most appropriate for you, your business, and given the knowledge you've gained by reading to this point, how you want to develop your own company. The goal was to provide a framework and basic understanding so that you could undertake your own due diligence and decide what was right for you. If you have questions, or would like to chat through your thought process as a way of coming to the right decision, by all means contact me.

This book has been written to outline the most common ways to raise funding for both new and existing businesses. In each case, I've attempted to give both an overview and some insights into the pros and cons of each funding method. It's intended, to be a good guide for more research and understanding related to each. My intention, is also to create a much richer and deeper book for each specific method. Obviously this will take some time, but it's a commitment I've made to my coaching clients, to the companies I advise, and to help the other entrepreneurs out there who have great ideas, great businesses and need some guidance to realize their visions.

Again, if you would like to reach out – Andrew (at) andrewive dot com

---

**** Your Executive Summary Free Gift
http://www.Andrewlve.com/executivesummarygift

Remember!

If you enjoyed this book and found it useful, there are two things you can do that will really help spread the word about it:

#1: You Can Write a Review

As an independent author, reviews are one of the most important ways I have to get the word out. Your review will encourage others to grab the book. You can share anything, but here are a few ideas:

- What you liked about the book

- What you didn't like about the book

- Your favorite, most useful chapter or part of the book

- Three things you are going to implement from the book

- The results you hope you are going to get or have already gotten from the book

Go to my author page here if you want to discuss any elements of the book or have follow up questions/thoughts (http://www.Amazon.com/author/andrewive)

If you do write a review, shoot me a note at andrew@andrewive.com (my personal email address) so I can thank you properly for your support.

When you do, also tell me a little about yourself (optional). Perhaps tell me about your business, your vision and your biggest goal. I'd love to hear from you.

#2: You can tell two Startups Friends about this Book

Why not tell two friends to check it out, send them a text or shoot them a message, maybe it will help them decide if they'd like to raise money for their business and how.

All the best and let me know if I can help you.

Andrew

**** Your Executive Summary Free Gift
http://www.AndrewIve.com/executivesummarygift

About the Author

A Brit living in Princeton, New Jersey, Andrew spent his early career at world class Fortune 100 marketing and innovative company Procter & Gamble but white space and high growth opportunities are Andrew's passion.

While at Harvard Business School, Andrew took a product idea sketch from his own teenage journal and starting from this new product idea, founded X-IT Products, which was named one of the United States 'Top 10 Start-ups' by a leading Entrepreneurial magazine and went on to win a 'Business Week' product design award. Andrew and his small team established a manufacturing facility in China and recruited a sales force to sell his first solo product into major US retailers. Andrew and the X-IT Product ladder were involved in a legal case that resulted in the largest corporate award in Virginia State history for his investors.

Andrew then founded a Silicon Valley company focused on solving data challenges between manufacturers and retailers. While CEO, Andrew built and led the executive team; Chaired the Board; raised $21M of capital, and began new partnerships and customer relationships with Home Depot, Black & Decker, BJs and others.

Recently, Andrew joined a small software/SAAS Silicon Valley based company and spent six years focused on driving strategic relationships, working with the core team to grow and prepare that company for an IPO in 2013.

Andrew has a passion for working with other entrepreneurs and enjoys innovation, developing new markets, new initiatives and high growth businesses opportunities. He has served on the Board of the Small Business Council of the Department of Trade and Industry advising the UK Government on startups and entrepreneurship; worked with the National Science Foundation evaluating business plans for grants and funding, the Investment Task Force (UK Government Task Force) and Centre for Policy Studies, Small Business Council (UK Think Tank focused on Small Business).

Andrew is married, has a daughter and the toughest 10 lb fluffy white dog resembling Snowy from the Tin-Tin books, and they all live in New Jersey.